Index

A FACILITATOR'S PRIMER ON ENTREPRENEURSHIP AND GROUP DYNAMISM

A FACILITATOR'S PRIMER
ON ENTREPRENEURSHIP AND GROUP DYNAMISM

(For Self Help Group Facilitators, Animators under DRDA, NGOs and CBOs)

LALDINLIANA

AKANSHA PUBLISHING HOUSE
NEW DELHI • GUWAHATI • VISAKHAPATNAM

AKANSHA PUBLISHING HOUSE
4649-B/21, Ansari Road
Darya Ganj, New Delhi - 110 002
Ph.: 23263193 / 9811582579 / 09435116718
Fax: 011-23263193
Email: ektabooks@yahoo.com
www.akanshapublishinghouse.com

A Facilitator's Primer on Entrepreneurship and Group Dynamism

First Edition, 2011
ISBN 978-81-8370-274-4

PRINTED IN INDIA

Published by Akansha Publishing House, New Delhi and Printed at Harmain Offset Press, Delhi.

To

Mom - Greatly missed

Contents

Foreword

India has witnessed a tremendous growth of sel fhelp groups (SHGs) in recent years; particularly the four southern States lead the country in micro-finance activities. They account for almost 54% of the SHGs but more importantly, for almost 75% of the bank credit. The microfinance movement started in the north-eastern regions around 1996-97, about eight years later when compared to many States in the country. Being under-banked, the north eastern States present a pathetic situation. The majority of the populations in these States have no access to any kind of banking services, not to speak of access to bank credit. This situation is well reflected in a simple statistic. While 35.5% households had access to banking services at all-India level in 2001, this figure was only 20.4% in the north eastern regions. Therefore, the banking services have not really been accessible to the majority of the population, mainly because of high transaction gaps, both for the bank and the borrower, amongst other things. Consequently, microfinance programmes and SHGs have gained immense relevance today. At the same time, we need to explore:

1) To what extent SHGs have helped the poor to get access to savings and credit?
2) What are the challenges and constraints faced by SHGs in accomplishing the target goals?

No doubt, the SHG programmes show a much skewed growth pattern in the country. The figures relating to distribution in the Region skewed very much in favour of Assam. Out of 34,238 SHGs in the region which received Rs. 101.89 crore as loans (31st March, 2005), over 90% belonged to Assam. Mizoram accounted for only 0.08% of total number of SHGs benefited in the region, with just 0.28% of total amount of loan dispensed. The NE States exhibited very insignificant figures despite the fact that they have substantial population size. Further, the distributions of SHGs are mostly clustered in the capital cities of these States.

Another concern is the quality of SHGs in terms of their governance, management and leadership. For example, in Andhra Pradesh which is the leading State in SHG formation, it was found that about 1/3rd of the SHGs were of unsatisfactory quality with regard to their organizational and financial management abilities. In many cases, it is found that SHG leaders have benefited relatively more from their SHGs financially, as well as development of individual abilities when compared to other members. Inadequate training and capacity building has been identified as one of the major factors responsible for low performance of SHGs. The success of the SHG movement in contributing to poverty alleviation and empowerment depends on the ability of members to take up innovative and productive livelihood or business ventures.

In this book, a sincere attempt has been made to touch up different aspects such as importance of participatory approach in rural development, the Swarnajayanti Gram Swarozgar Yojana (SGSY), dynamics of entrepreneurship, practical facilitation for entrepreneurial development of SHGs as micro-enterprises, creativity development and so on. The book has been written in a lucid style with many self-assessment exercises. Books of this kind will go a long way in strengthening the participatory approach which is considered an essential prerequisite for achieving all round development, particularly in rural India.

I congratulate Shri Laldinliana for authoring this book which is a crucial and timely intervention.

NVR Jyoti Kumar
Professor and Head
Dept. of Commerce
Mizoram University
Aizawl

Dated 1st January 2011

Preface

"I WILL CONSIDER YOU successful if you start off with your own enterprise, not if you get yourself government employed" were the words of my professor at Loyola College, Chennai before we wind up the entrepreneurship specialization electives. His message was simple, yet intriguing. Entrepreneurship was conferred to me as a mission by whom I consider one of the commerce department's pinnacle. Well, things do go full circle, or rather, overlapping as I went back to my alma mater again as an officer of State Institute of Rural Development. A warm wide grin crosses the face of the senior Professor Janakidoss as I was making a remark before the Loyola M.Com. students while giving a seminar, that I came back, not only as a government employee, but also as an entrepreneur and more importantly, as a faculty who taught entrepreneurship. He remembered!

My education as an entrepreneurship "specialist" met, or rather collide with veracity as I went rural. Remnants of defunct Self Help Groups show strains of hard reality- of wrong tools of motivation, of entrepreneurial deficiency, of sick group management and of cruel facilitation. Maybe, just maybe, we can go an extra mile had we a better animation and facilitation faculty. I am convinced that I have attained the 'A-ha' stage when I saw almost all my entrepreneurship trainees in the 6 districts come home with more than Rs.

500, a reward for group entrepreneurship exercise we had with Rs. 100 as seed capital in just 3 days! The acid-test works. And to add fuel to fire, I had the chance to witness and experience the Kurnool's Social Mobilization Experimentation and Learning Centre (SMELC) at Andhra Pradesh. An institution enacted and operated by a federation of women SHGs shine as a testimony that SHG model is an answer for many mizo rural poor. With the right motivation and tool, failure-prone self help groups can morph to prominent micro-enterprises, not only as self sustainment, but a large chunk in the State's economy.

This book is sewn together from bits-and-pieces of various addresses as a sincere attempt to rekindle the SHG Facilitators' dynamism; a chronicle of thoughts and insights of revered entrepreneurship gurus and writers; a journal of leadership drills and maneuvers; a primer of practical tools coined by thinkers and doers. And I stand, not as an authority, but a humble compiler.

—***Laldinliana***

PART ONE
THEORETICAL

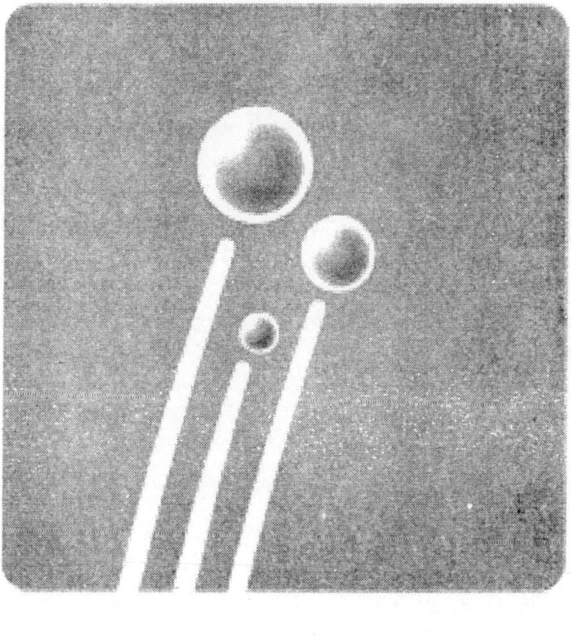

1

Participatory Approach in Development

1.1 Backdrop – A Complimentary Retrospection

Alleviation of rural poverty has been one of the primary objectives of planned development in India. Ever since the inception of planning, the policies and the programmes have been designed and redesigned with this holy crusade. The problem of rural poverty was brought into a sharper focus during the Sixth Plan. Prominent programmes like Integrated Rural Development Programme (IRDP), Training of Rural Youth for Self Employment (TRYSEM), Development of Women and Children in Rural Areas (DWCRA), Jawahar Rozgar Yojana (JRY- which is basically a merged wage employment programme of NREP and RLEGP). During the Ninth Plan period, several anti-poverty programmes have been restructured to enhance the efficiency of the Programmes for providing increased benefits to the rural poor. Self Employment Programmes have been enhanced by merging the Integrated Rural Development Programme (IRDP), the Development of Women and Children in Rural Areas (DWCRA), the Supply of Improved Tool-Kits to Rural Artisans (SITRA), Training of Rural Youth for Self Employment (TRYSEM), the Ganga Kalyan Yojana (GKY) and the Million Wells Scheme (MWS) into a holistic selfemployment scheme called Swarnjayanti Gram Swarozgar Yojana (SGSY). Other flagship programmes of the Ministry of Rural Development include the Indira Awas Yojana (IAY), Integrated Wasteland Development Programme (IWDP), Pradhan Mantri Gram Sadak Yojana (PMGSY- dealing with rural connectivity) etc. These schemes and programmes are no strangers to our State.

1.2 Scenario Shift

With so much given by the Central policy makers, much is left to be pondered upon in Mizoram. April 19th 2007 saw an event which was unprecedented in the Mizo history in the form of a mass demonstration of Zoram Kuthnathawktu Pawl (ZPK) in which a gathering of poverty-stricken rural farmers shout out their common grief. Their cries reflect the pleas and challenges of their rights deprived. An invoked demonstration which reflect the awakening for the need of 'people's participation' and empowerment at the core of which stands the bottom line — the rights of the grassroots stakeholders.

Where do we go wrong? Where do we fall short? Pointing fingers is not much of a solution as it is. We need to take the rural development programmes more seriously. After all, it is only appropriate that we, the scholars of the State take more intense probe into the projects undertaken to alleviate the rural areas.

To understand the rural programmes, we have to look into the anatomy of every project. For every project, a management guru would hold out the banner of *Planning, Organizing, Staffing, Directing and Controlling.* In rural development programmes, these parameters too hold true in a parallel line. The life-segments and application of programmes do run on these principles. The following diagram would give an illustrative understanding:

The important dimension of programmes in rural development is its stakeholders. As Mizoram does not run with the Panchayati Raj Institution (PRI) system, the linkage of **stakeholders** can be illustrated as:

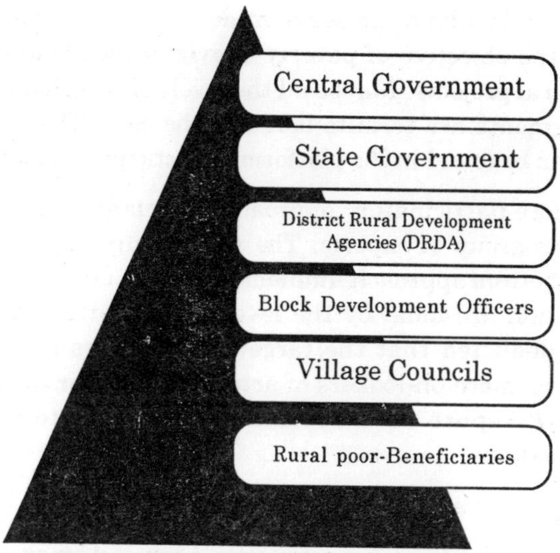

From the above representation, we can see the main sponsoring/ funding entity is the Central Government as Ministry of Rural Development (MoRD). Depending upon the programmes, the State will have to contribute a ratio to the total budget known as 'State Matching Share'. The DRDAs are the district functionaries and their basic function is to disburse the development funds to the block level. At the block level, the Block Development Officers are the authority in implementing programmes. Again, the order is not uniform in all programmes. They, in turn, delegate the Village Councils at village level in the implementation of the projects at grass root level. The last stakeholders are the ultimate beneficiaries — the rural poor. Management and evaluations are done at each level as required by the guidelines of the concerned programmes.

1.3 Transition to Participatory Approach

So then, at what level of the stakeholders do we see the shortfall? At which life-segment do we see the crisis which dazed the objective of poverty-alleviation we hold so dear with rural projects? Maybe all the levels of stakeholders and life-segments are termite-bored at the core. The elixir we need can be found in the platform of Participatory Approach.

Before participatory approach, the planning is done by the elite group of experts. The very nature of planning is top-to-bottom approach. Implementation, management and evaluation are done by the level functionaries. It can be safely deducted that the target beneficiaries are the by-standers, mere on-lookers of activities done for their sake. CIRDAP report 1984 identifies 7 barriers to people's participation-

1. Easy availability of grants and subsidies
2. Prejudice and discrimination against women
3. Illiteracy and lack of awareness
4. Factionalism and heterogeneity of population
5. Disparities in wealth and social studies
6. Interference by politicians
7. Misunderstanding about the motivation and objectives of people's organization.

Such practice of project implementation cannot bring forth a holistic development in its target groups, especially in rural areas. Many poor people's realities are local, complex, diverse, dynamic and unpredictable. The values and preferences of poor rural people typically contrast with those of the better-off outsiders and professionals. Local people are themselves diverse, with sharp contrast of preferences and priorities by age, gender, social and ethic group and wealth. Without the rural poor's participation and commitment in every segment of rural projects, rural upliftment projects broadcast an image so much alike the proverbial "giving a fish instead of teaching how to fish". Depth development can never be achieved as long as the rural communities are nullified with easy subsidies and grants. Yes, the roads and assets created are not theirs; they have not asked for it; they have not planned for it; they have no hand in it. So who are they to take care of it! All they know is that the government officials came and told them they need this-and-that and then it was done. Thus, a paradigm change is called for in the development sphere, a transition from the frail extractive system of existing rural alleviation to the more dynamic and catholic system of participatory approach. As often said in marketing management, marketing begins and ends with consumers, so is in rural development in a transcending form. *Rural development is all about the grass-root beneficiaries, the rural poor. Thus, rural development should begin and end with people's participation.*

1.4 The Gospel to Rural Development Programmes

What is participation that we spoke with such reverence? Participation is basically a political process concerned with redistribution of administrative and financial powers and legal information in a society with the local whose involvement is sought. South Asian scholars in the UNU Programme have defined participation in relation to the emerging praxis as "Participation is democracy...Participation means commitment to a more egalitarian society which permits equal access to resources not only to landbut also to food, education, health and other basic human rights.

When formal power is in the hands of a few, their power are grossly misused; participation means building countervailing power which leads to a healthier democracy." Basically, people's participation in rural development means a non-passive involvement of the rural beneficiaries at every level and segment of the programmes- in planning, implementing, management, monitoring and evaluation (or reflection, as Ms. Sushmita Chuk, IAS, Jt. Secretary of MoRD passionately stated in our interaction at NIRD-NERC 12th October 2007). The rationale of participatory approach can be summarized out as follows:

1. Reduction of development cost to the government or NGOs in planning, implementing and monitoring
2. Increase in the perceived and actual benefits to people participating in the programme
3. Correction of mistakes made by the project authority in designing various structures
4. Reaching the benefits of developmental programmes to all legitimate claimants.
5. Decrease in perpetual dependence of the people on the government and NGOs, thereby making the programme self-sustaining and the rural locals self-reliant
6. Gaining accesses to and control of resources and mobilization of indigenous technologies, designed to fit the mould of their specific local scenario
7. Empowerment of the people of their rights and duties
8. Ease in implementation of programmes with the participation of the locals

9. Sense of ownership and belongingness induced to the beneficiaries by their participation.

1.5 Realm of Theory or Manifestation of Reality

Much is left to be said as far as participation is concerned. It is worthy to note that participatory approach led to prominent successes in various implications. Take the case of Comilla experiment in East Bengal during the 1950s; The Grameen Bank in Bangladesh; Bhoomi Sena in India and the Aga Khan Rural Support Programme in Gilgit and Skardu of northern Pakistan. Orangi Project in Karachi, Pakistan and Working Women's Forum in Tamil Nadu, India will have lots to speak about. And now, the UPA brain-child, the goliath of all rural development programmes incarnated as an Act by the Parliament of Indian Union bear the insignia of people's participation as a mandatory requirement. The haloed National Rural Employment Guarantee Programme (NREGP), which was flagged off on Feb. 2, 2006 will bring the participatory approach to a new higher ground. Dr. Raghuvansh Prasad Singh, Minister for Rural Development, recently expressed that, implementation of NREGP in 200 districts in its first phase, has generated 65.35 crore person-days of employment and more than 7 lakh works (up to Feb'07) have been taken up, to create national assets. NREGA's, made a good beginning in tackling the challenges of poverty, unemployment and building rural infrastructure. The first phase includes the Saiha and Lawngtlai District. In the Union Budget 2007-08, the finance minister allocated a sum of Rs 120 billion for NREGS while expanding the scheme to 330 districts from the current level of 200 districts. This second phase embraces Lunglei and Champhai District. Now, the whole nation started implementing this Act-fortified programme. The NREGA makes it mandatory that the planning of 'shelf of projects' will be done at grass-root level. This means that planning will be a bottom-to-top approach where the Gram Sabha or village gathering will identify their own needs and works to be taken up for the guaranteed wage employment. The grass root beneficiaries (rural adult citizens) themselves apply for job-cards and express their application of willingness to work. The works will be assessed by the locally created body called Village Monitoring Committee comprising of prominent and trustworthy locals. Without their consent, the village level project implementing agency (Village Council, in the case of Mizoram) cannot draw money from the block level authority, the Programme Officer (BDOs in Mizoram). Furthermore, the Act made it compulsory to conduct Social Audit twice a year. The social audit is the checking and discussion by the public meeting of local citizens regarding every aspect of the NREGP. All the financial documents, assets created, muster roll engaged, wage paid etc. will be discussed in detail by the rural citizens themselves and their findings and reports will be detailed to the block level authority. To sum up the NREGP, people's participation is the main ingredient in planning, implementing, monitoring and evaluation. The violation of the mandate set by the Act will thus be a criminal offense to the Nation itself.

1.6 The Mission

The central actors in the participatory process are the *hitherto excluded,* that is the poor, the deprived and the underprivileged rural poor, who have traditionally lacked opportunities to participate in social processes benefiting them. Three central elements can be identified in participatory processes, namely-

1. *Animation*: assisting the people to build up their intellectual capacities and knowledge of how to think, reflect and act autonomously;

2. *Facilitation*: assisting the people to acquire practical skills (such as technical, managerial) and literacy, to improve their access to resources and where necessary,

even to create space for people's actions by playing a protective or a nursing role in the initial stages;

3. *Progressive Redundancy*: making conscious efforts to ensure a progressive reduction in the need of external animation and facilitation, an ability to phase out, leaving to the people to manage their own affairs.

It is our ethical and social obligation as learned scholars, to empower the rural locals to take a leash of their lives towards better living. Development cannot go limping. It has to take strides as so much is at stake. A single-winged flight is not the answer to attain the vision of utopia. Even if an Act enforces a programme, there will be loop-holes. That is where we, the scholars have to step in and plug the holes. We cannot afford to have the rural poor deprived of their rights and claims which is rightfully theirs. Instead, we need to teach them "how to fish", to have a sense of ownership and involvement in their own planned benefits. After all, the 500 BC thinker Heraclitus stated "Nothing is permanent but change". So whose reality counts? It is time we put the last first and make rural development programmes something which is all about the rural poor.

2

A Brief Overview on Swarnajayanti Gram Swarozgar Yojana

2.1 Objective

A life of dignity is the right of every citizen. Poverty is an obstruction to a dignified life. Self-employment is a significant step to have sustained incomes and remove the shackles of poverty. Earlier programme like IRDP were good but were not adequate to meet all the requirements. Governments have now introduced an effective Self-Employment programme 'Swarnajayanti Gram Swarozgar', or SGSY.

Under the SGSY, assistance is given to the poor families living below the poverty line in rural areas for taking up self employment. The persons taking up Self-Employment are called swarozgaris. They may take up the activity either individually or in Groups, called the Self-Help Groups. For successful Self-Employment, it is necessary to take up the right activity. For this purpose, 4 to 5 activities are selected in each Block with the help of officials, non-officials and the

Bankers. These are called 'Key Activities', and should be such that they give the Swarozgaris an income of Rs. 2000 per month, net of Bank loan repayment.

Quite often, in villages, people have skills. If any BPL person feel that he/she can gainfully take up any activity he/she should immediately approach NGOs facilitating SHGs or the BDO or the Branch Manager of the nearest Bank.

Effective Self-Employment not only means choosing the Right activity but also carrying out the activity in the Right manner. Self-Employment involves procurement of raw material, production, marketing of goods and dealing with finance. A single Swarozgari may not be able to do all this by himself/herself. It is therefore advisable for the Swarozgaris to form Groups – the Self-Help Groups. SGSY actively promotes Self-Help Groups.

2.2 Self-Help Group

A Self- Help Group (SHG) may generally consist of 10-20 persons. However, in difficult areas like deserts, hills and areas with scattered and sparse population and in case of minor irrigation and disabled persons, this number may be from 5.20. The difficult areas have to be identified by the state level SGSY Committee.

2.3 Compositions of the Self-Help Group

Generally all members of the Group should belong to families below the poverty. However, if necessary, a maximum of 20%, and in exceptional cases, where essentially required, upto a maximum of 30% of the members in a Group may be from families marginally above the poverty line, living continuously with BPL families and if they are acceptable to BPL members of the Group. The APL members of Group will not be eligible for subsidy under the scheme and shall not become office bearers (Group leader, assistant group leader or treasurer) of the group. The BPL families must actively participate in the management and decision-making which should not be entirely in the hands of APL families.

In case of disabled persons a group may comprises of persons with diverse disabilities or group may comprise of both disabled and non-disabled persons below the poverty line.

2.4 Subsidy Norms for SHGs and Disabled Persons

Subsidy under the SGSY will be uniform at 30% of the project cost, subject to a maximum of Rs. 7500/-. In respect of SC/STs and disabled persons however, these will be 50% and Rs. 10,000/- respectively. For group of Swarozgaris (SHGs), the subsidy would be 50% of the project cost subject to per capital subsidy of Rs. 10,000/- or monetary limit on subsidy for irrigation projects.

2.5 SHG Membership Criteria

- Persons from the poorest household & Bottom of the Pyramid
- Only one person from a family
- Homogenous people, residing in the same village/area
- Generally, if women , married are preferable
- 18 to 60 years of age and willing to follow the rules of the SHG
- Preference is to be given to include the socially disadvantaged like widows, STs, women headed households, landless & handicapped.

2.6 Rules and Regulations of a SHG

- Group meetings are to be held on fixed days or dates, and at fixed time.

- Groups can collect fine from the member-absentees
- Groups should have two third (or 75%) presence of members in the meeting for taking important decisions.
- Group can select the leaders for their group and term of leadership should be specified.
- Group's bank account should be operated jointly by the SHG leaders.
- Group's books of accounts should be audited by the internal audit team of CBOs / NGOs / external auditors at the end of the financial year.
- Group leaders should readout the financial position of the group (total funds, outstanding as loans with members, loan balance payable to the bank, amount to be remitted to the bank, cash on hand, bank balance and any defaults by members) at the end of the group meeting and should specify who would go to the bank for remitting the collections.
- All financial transactions of the members be held in public in the group meetings only.
- All decisions taken in the group meeting are properly to be recorded in the SHG's minute book, read at the end and signed by the members present.
- Group can decide about how much to save per member (e.g not less than Rs.20 per fortnight or Rs.10 per week), what is the maximum size of its internal loan, its interest, subscription amount and terms of repayment.

2.7 Role of SHG Leaders

- To convene the group meetings and facilitate the proceedings.
- To dele gate the group tasks to members and nurture them.

- To write the group's account books and minutes / resolution book.
- To attend the training programmes and to share the inputs with the group.
- To facilitate the SHG's access to the bank and other government programs.
- To resolve the conflicts and build trust among the members,
- To handle the money in the group meetings (collection of savings, subscription, internal loan repayments and disbursal of credit).
- To sign the bank cheques and operate the Group's SB account jointly.
- To inform the financial position of the group to members in the meeting and ensure financial transparency.

2.8 Role of Members

- To attend the group meetings regularly.
- To participate actively in the group proceedings.
- To remit the savings, loan repayments and subscription in meetings.
- To verify the resolution passed & sign in the resolution book.
- To go to the bank along with the leader in rotation.
- To participate in the training programmes.

2.9 Role of Field Staff

- Forming the new SHGs by enrolling the eligible members.

- Nurturing the SHGs by giving periodical training.
- Developing the SHG leaders for facilitating the SHGs.
- Facilitating SHGs to set SMART (Specific, Measurable, Achievable, Relevant and Time bound) goals for every year.
- Monitoring the key performance indicators (whether meetings held, Attendance, Number of members saved, Amount of savings, Loan repayment against the demand for the month, Drop-outs if any, Social issues addressed by the SHG) of SHGs every month.
- Inculcating the habit of planning in SHGs.
- Facilitating credit access to the SHGs with the bank.
- Ensuring the SHG members go to the bank every month in rotation.
- Reviewing the maintenance of account books at the SHG level every month.
- Maintaining a simple MIS (Management Information System) database on their SHG bank linkage program.
- Creating linkages between the mainstream institutions (marketing, training and technology development institutions) and the SHGs.
- Enabling the SHGs to solve the conflicts among the members by themselves.
- Guiding SHGs to reach the sustainability.
- Facilitating SHGs to practice leadership rotation every two years.
- Evaluating the SHGs at the end of every year and recommending the best performing SHGs to the management for awards.

2.10 Group Functions

- Convening of group meetings.
- Inculcating the habit of savings and mobilizing savings from members.
- Lending to the members out of the group funds for meeting the member's credit needs.
- Building the capacity of the members by giving opportunities to them to participate in various group activities.
- Providing a forum to members to share their problems and enabling them to find a solution to their problems.
- Maintaining SHG's books of accounts and resolution (Minutes) book.
- Planning and organizing need based social and community development programs.
- Creating linkages with the other developmental agencies so as to solicit support for their own and their social/ community development.
- Exerting peer pressure (ability of applying social pressure by all the members to enforce the sanctions on members violating the group rule) on the members, who tend to violate the rules of SHG.
- Facilitating learning new things by members through training.

2.11 Group Meetings

- The SHG should conduct its group meetings on fixed days /dates at fixed times convenient to the members.
- Fortnightly meetings are better, as it enables frequent face to face interaction among members, which will

result in better understanding among the members. One meeting shall focus on financial issues and the other shall focus on social issues.

- The group meeting shall be conducted as per the agenda namely, prayer, pledge, attendance, review of previous minutes of the meeting, collection of savings, subscription, internal loan / bank loan repayments, discussion on credit sanctions, delivery of credit, planning for village development activities, passing the resolutions by recording them in the resolution (Minutes) note, reading out and getting the members signature in the resolution note.
- By observing the Group meetings keenly, one can know the group dynamism (how the members express their opinions freely, how the view of other members are sought and valued while arriving at a decision by the group and how the leaders encourage other members to take responsibility) in the SHG, which is a key factor for the cohesiveness of the group.

2.12 SHG Funds Management

- The SHG collects the savings from their members in the group meetings.
- Fortnightly savings is a better option, as it will be easy for the group members to save in small amounts.
- SHG rotates the savings among its members as internal loans for various purposes.
- The purpose will be prioritized by the group in the meeting. The interest on internal loan collected from the members will be a major source of revenue for the SHGs.
- All the funds are properly accounted for in specified books of accounts of the SHG.

- The SHG maintains the savings bank account in its name, in a bank of its choice. The account is to be operated jointly by the SHG leaders.
- The group will maintain a nominal balance Rs.50 to Rs.100 only as cash at hand and the rest will be deposited in the bank.
- The members who have opted to save more, are not granted with any special benefits, except to the proportionate increased share in the dividend distributions made out of the interest income, at a later date.
- The Facilitator shall not handle the SHG's money.
- SHG leaders should not collect any money privately from the members on behalf of the group.
- After a period of 3 to 5 years, the SHG shall review its repayment term, maximum loan size norms and can introduce appropriate changes in their rules & regulations, as decided by the group.

2.13 Grading of Self Help Groups

Self Help Groups need to pass a stage called 'Gradings' in order to qualify them for bank credit. The following is the general key points and themes SHGs are graded on

Sl. No.	*Category*	*Criteria*	*Mark*	*Key*
1	COMPOSITION	Membership is homogeneous No homogeneity in membership	10 5	The rating is based on the judgment of assessing official
		One year and above	10	There is no need to

(Contd...)

Sl. No.	*Category*	*Criteria*	*Mark*	*Key*
2	AGE OF THE GROUP	Six months and above but less than a year	5	evaluate an SHG if it is less than six month old (ignore marginal shortfalls upto 1 month)
3	WEEKLY GROUP MEETINGS	Four meetings per month 2-3 meetings per month 8 1 meeting per month	10 5	The total number of meetings conducted during the last 3 months may be divided by 3 to arrive at average no. of group meetings.
4	ATTENDANCE	More than 90% Between 70% and 90% Less than 70%	10 5 3	See explanation 1 at the end. Written in detail 10
5	MINUTES BOOK	Maintained, but not in detail Participation by only a few members	5 5	Peruse of minutes book pertaining to meetings held during the last 3 months.
6	PARTICIPATION IN GROUP DISCUSSION	Participation by majority of members	10	Peruse minutes book (if rating is 10 for item 5) Observe during a couple of group meeting Interact with members

(Contd...)

Sl. No.	*Category*	*Criteria*	*Mark*	*Key*
7	SAVINGS (FREQUENCY)	4 times a month (by majority members)	10	**Step 1 :** Take the average no. of members making saving during last 3 months.
		4 times a month (but not by majority)	8	**Step 2 :** Compare this with the total no. of members
		2-3 times a month (by majority members)	8	**Step 3 :** Majority mean > 60%
		2-3 times a month (but not by majority	5	**Step 4 :** For average no. of meeting, follow rating given for item 3 above.
		1 time a month day (by majority members)	3	**Note :** Please see explanation 2 at the end.
		1 time a month (but not by majority)	1	
8	SAVINGS & LOAN RECOVERY (MODE OF COLLECTION)	Collected in group meetings	10	Ascertain form group leaders and members in this regard also, peruse minutes book.
		House - to house collection	5	
9	STYLE OF FUNCTIONING AND GROUP DECISIONS	Democratic and Transparent	10	Peruse minutes book, Interact with members, Observe in few group meetings, Ascertain whether periodical elections are conducted for
		Decisions taken by few dominant member / members / group leaders	0	

(Contd...)

Sl. No.	*Category*	*Criteria*	*Mark*	*Key*
				the leadership and whether all decisions are in group meetings and on democratic lines.
		Selection of borrowers in group meetings	2	Ascertain the position from group leaders/ members
		Sanction and disbursement of loans in group meetings	2	Peruse minutes book (Each item will get marks shown against it, if the conditions are satisfied)
		Loan terms and conditions discussed in group meetings and recorded in minutes	2	
		Utilisation of loans reviewed regularly in group meetings	2	
10	SANCTION AND DISBURSEMENT OF LOANS	Recovery of loans reviewed regularly ingroup meetings.	2	
		Uniform rate irrespective of source of funds	5	
		Different rates depending on source of funds	3	
		Interest rates vary according to the purpose of loan	5	

(Contd...)

Sl. No.	*Category*	*Criteria*	*Mark*	*Key*
11	INTEREST ON SHG LOANS	Uniform interest rate for all purposes	3	Peruse loan register. Ascertain from group leaders / members
12	UTILISATION OF SAVING FOR LOANING	Above 80%	10	Compare savings outstanding on a given date with loans outstanding on the same date to obtain the percentage. Nil mark for utilisation of savings below 50%
		Above 50% and upto 80%	4	
13	RECOVERY OF LOANS	Dues not recovered in respect of 10% or less of total no. of loan accounts	10	Even one installment unpaid without authorisation by the group is treated as dues not recovered. Count such accounts and compare them with total no. of loan a/c. Also, peruse minutes book for authorisation for non-payment
		Dues not recovered between 10% and 30% of total no.of loan accounts.	4	
		Attendance-cum-minutes book	3	

(Contd...)

Sl. No.	*Category*	*Criteria*	*Mark*	*Key*
		Savings Register	3	
		Loan Ledger	3	
14	BOOKS OF ACCOUNTS	Bank Passbook	1	Each record / register, if maintained properly and upto date, will get marks shown against each.
15	BYLAWS / GROUP RULES	Known to all members	10	Ascertain from the member through interaction
		Known to most of the members	5	
		Not known to many members	0	
	Total Marks		**150**	

1. SHG scoring more than 120 marks out of maximum of 150 marks could be chosen for credit linkage
2. SHG scoring less than 120 marks will have to be further developed before linkage. The areas for taken up after 3 months.

3

Linking SGSY with Entrepreneurship

The SGSY theme is that the Self Help Groups (SHGs) should be able to sustain themselves through effective economic activities and management. That is where entrepreneurial development is much called for.

In Alapakkam Village of Kattankolathur Panchayat Union women members have joined together and started one Magalir Malligai Mandram during April 1992. Consequent on the introduction of SGSY Scheme this Self Help Group has opened a Savings Bank Account in Indian Bank, Ozhalur.

> Since this Group was started as early 1992 Revolving fund of Rs. 25,000/- was sanctioned on 04.02.1999. Initially the members of the group preparing and selling varieties of snacks and they found a very good market among the customers. When they approached the DRDA for developing their Economic Activity. The DRDA made arrangements for running a canteen at SIRD, Maraimalai Nagar Campus and sanctioned a sum of Rs. 1,60,000/- under Economic Assistance with 50% Subsidy of Rs. 80,000/- on 29.12.2001 and the SHGs members have started a Canteen on 04.01.2002. This canteen is exclusively run by these Malligai Magalir Women Self Help Group to the entire

satisfaction of the Officers and the regular customers of Trainees.

Several Officials including Government of India representatives has appreciated the Self Help Groups function.

So far this Self Help Group have repaid the loan amount to the tune of Rs. 47,700/-. The SHGs members have also earning a sum of Rs. 2000/- per month by each SHGs member besides giving employment for 6 more women workers through this canteen. Before starting this canteen the income of the the members from other sources was only Rs. 100 to Rs. 500 per month depending upon the labour work. Thus the Malligai Magalir Women Self Group have achieved a great success in catering field and benefited by the SGSY Scheme.

The above case demonstrates how entrepreneurship does bring about economic development to the members of SHGs. Yet it is sad to say that the hypothesis in Mizoram is that majority of the Self Help Groups failed because they miss the very crucial element- the 'self help' element. Much of the SHG population kicks off with the main aim of subsidy and grants. This alone contradicts the basic yet unsung entrepreneurial trait. To help the SHGs, the role of the facilitator will thus be crucial in developing an entrepreneurial spirit in the SHGs to bring about a change and enhancement in the standard of living of the group members and the society, ultimately.

Sushila Selp-Help Group was formed in village Faringola under Project Pahla Kadam (ADB small grant program).There are 12 members in the group who contribute Rs 30 per month.

Azad India Foundation organized training in detergent and agarbatti (incense) stick making from Khadi Gram Commission for the group members. The group members then decided to start agarbatti making on small scale. They pooled their resources and bought raw material from Kishanganj and Siliguri.

After the incense sticks were ready the main problem was of marketing. The president of the Group Sushila along with her daughter Kalyani started selling to the paan shops, house to house within the village and extended family. They earned profit of Rs 100 which gave them hope and strength for the future. Again they bought raw material and devised new strategy. Now they do two type of packeting -one rupee and 10 rupees. One rupee packets are sold within the village and ten rupee packets are given to small shops outside the village etc.

They also have started giving money on interest to women within the group and village also. Earlier it was Rs 2 per month now they have raised it to Rs 10 per month within the group and Rs 15 for the women other than group.

4

Facilitation

Facilitation may be defined as helping a group to accomplish its goals. There are a wide range of perspectives about the ideal nature and values of facilitation, much as there are a wide range of perspectives about the ideal nature and values of leadership. For example, some facilitators may believe that facilitation should always be highly democratic in nature and that anything other than democratic is not facilitation at all. Others may believe that facilitation can be quite directive, particularly depending on the particular stage of development of the group.

The practice usually is carried out by someone who has strong knowledge and skills regarding group dynamics and processes (process skills). Effective facilitation might also involve strong knowledge and skills about the particular topic or content that the group is addressing in order to reach its goals (content skills).

4.1 Why Facilitation?

Effectively facilitated groups produce higher quality work, and build a broader base of support for timely implementation. Facilitation is particularly helpful when the membership of the group is diverse in knowledge, background, and interests; where there are existing or potential conflicts among the parties; and when the topics are complex. Facilitation is such a necessity in the context of Mizoram, reason being multifold. Starting from the motivation of SHGs, the animation is done using subsidies as lure. That may be the reason why much of the groups formed defunct after receiving subsidies. Had the groups been facilitated in the field of entrepreneurship, notable SHGs should already be in existence. In a State like Mizoram, where we find a highly sociable population, facilitation with expertise in group dynamics and management would contribute much towards more successful group function.

4.2 Why a Facilitator?

An experienced facilitator helps the group stay focused on its tasks, explore the situation more fully, minimize interpersonal conflict unrelated to task, work through conflict that is central to the work of the group and build openness and support within the group. The facilitator's work allows the group leader to more fully participate in the work of the group.

4.3 Facilitator Competencies from EDGES published by ICA: Canada

1. The Facilitator is effective in using core methods (distinguishes process from content).
2. The Facilitator carefully manages the client relationship and prepares thoroughly (scoping).
3. The Facilitator uses time and space intentionally.
4. The Facilitator is skillful in evoking participation and creativity.

5. The Facilitator is practiced in honoring the group and affirming its wisdom.
6. The Facilitator is capable of maintaining objectivity.
7. The Facilitator is skilled in reading the underlying dynamics of the group.
8. The Facilitator orchestrates the event drama.
9. The Facilitator releases blocks to the process.
10. The Facilitator is adroit in adapting to the changing situation.
11. The Facilitator assumes responsibility for the group journey.
12. The Facilitator can produce powerful documentation.
13. The Facilitator demonstrates professionalism, selfconfidence, and authenticity.
14. The Facilitator maintains personal integrity.

4.4 Characteristics of a Facilitator

One who is willing to commit to a style of

1. "asking" rather than "telling."
2. paying personal compliments.
3. willing to spend time in building relationships rather than being always task-oriented.
4. initiating conversation rather than waiting for someone else to.
5. asking for other's opinions rather than always having to offer their own.
6. negotiating rather than dictating decision-making.
7. listening without interrupting.

8. Emoting but able to be restrained when the situation requires it.
9. drawing energy from outside themselves rather than from within.
10. basing decisions upon intuitions rather than having to have facts.
11. has sufficient self-confidence that they can look someone in the eye when talking to them.
12. more persuasive than sequential.
13. more enthusiastic than systematic.
14. more outgoing than serious.
15. more like a coach than a scientist.
16. more like a counselor than a sergeant.
17. is naturally curious about people, things and life in general.
18. can keep the big picture in mind while working on the micro level.
19. In the final analysis, anyone can be a facilitator who is willing to be flexible and not bound by, a slave to, and their natural social style.

4.5 Facilitator's Self Help Group Do's and Don'ts

- Ensure that the group meeting is used as a platform to develop members skills (esp. communication).
- Facilitate the members to do one task each (viz. Singing prayer song, Oath taking, Attendance taking, Cash collection, Record keeping, Resolution writing, Reading the minutes, Obtaining the signatures in the minutes book and Opting to go to bank for remitting the group money) during the group meeting.

- When one member violates the rule (not repaying the loan instalment), all members should exert pressure and ask that member.
- Facilitate all members to involve themselves in taking decisions.
- All cash transactions have to be carried out and recorded in the books of a/cs during the group meeting to maintain the transparency.
- Encourage SHGs to celebrate their anniversary and let them reflect on their achievements and plan for the future.
- Do not force anything on the SHG. Give them choice. Explain the pros and cons of each option. Facilitate them to choose their option.
- Do not talk to the office bearers of the group alone while taking a crucial decision. Have a feedback from the members.
- Do not encourage the system of handling money & keeping the SHG account by the same person.
- Do not encourage the situation, where same office bearers of the SHGs continue to hold office for years together.
- Do not encourage the GROUP activity, unless the SHG is stabilized well and it has a good facilitating support of a NGO.
- Do not allow the SHG to distribute the loan equally to all members.
- Do not allow the SHGs with political or communal backing.

5

Group Dynamics

When people work in groups, there are two quite separate issues involved. The first is the task and the problems involved in getting the job done. Frequently this is the only issue which the group considers. The second is the process of the group work itself: the mechanisms by which the group acts as a unit and not as a loose rabble. However, without due attention to this process the value of the group can be diminished or even destroyed; yet with a little explicit management of the process, it can enhance the worth of the group to be many times the sum of the worth of its individuals. It is this synergy which makes group work attractive in corporate organization despite the possible problems (and time spent) in group formation.

The key is that the group should be viewed as an important resource whose maintenance must be managed just like any other resource and that this management should be undertaken by the group itself so that it forms a normal part of the group's activities.

5.1 What is Group Process?

A group of people working in the same room, or even on a common project, does not necessarily invoke the group process. If the group is managed in a totally autocratic manner, there may be little opportunity for interaction relating to the work; if there is faction within the group, the process may never evolve. On the other hand, the group process may be utilized by normally distant individuals working on different projects.

In simple terms, the group process leads to a spirit of cooperation, coordination and commonly understood procedures and mores. If this is present within a group of people, then their performance will be enhanced by their mutual support (both practical and moral). If you think this is a nebulous concept when applied to the world of industry, consider the opposite effect that a self-opinionated, cantankerous loud-mouth would have on your performance and then contrast that to working with a friendly, open, helpful associate.

5.2 Why a Group?

It is always inspiring to reflect on the root beginning of one of the most successful 'self help' group – Alcoholic Anonymous. Bill Wilson was a budding businessman when he struggled with wine, devastating his career and life in general. After winning the hard bout with alcoholism, he went on again on business trip. That trip proved to be a difficult one. Depressed and disappointed, he stopped by a wine shop. The music, laughter and tinkling of wine bottles made him think "I need a drink". It was then when he realized - he doesn't need a drink, he need another drunkard! In a group, one finds consistency, multifold development, security, strength, belongingness and pride. Groups are particularly good at combining talents and providing innovative solutions to possible unfamiliar problems; in cases where there is no well established approach/procedure, the wider skill and knowledge set of the group has a distinct advantage over that of the individual.

A group can be seen as a self managing unit. The range of skills provided by its members and the self monitoring which each group performs makes it a reasonably safe recipient for delegated responsibility. Even if a problem could be decided by a single person, there are two main benefits in involving the people who will carry out the decision. Firstly, the motivational aspect of participating in the decision will clearly enhance its implementation. Secondly, there may well be factors which the implementer understands better than the single person who could supposedly have decided alone.

More indirectly, if the lowest echelons of the workforce each become trained, through participation in group decision making, in an understanding of the group's objectives and work practices, then each will be better able to solve work-related problems in general. Further, they will also individually become a safe recipient for delegated authority which is exemplified in the celebrated right of Japanese car workers to halt the production line.

From the individual's point of view, there is the added incentive that through belonging to a group each can participate in achievements well beyond his/her own individual potential. Less idealistically, the group provides an environment where the individual's self-perceived level of responsibility and authority is enhanced, in an environment where accountability is shared: thus providing a perfect motivator through enhanced self-esteem coupled with low stress.

5.3 Group Development

It is common to view the development of a group as having four stages:

1. Forming
2. Storming
3. Norming

4. Performing.

Forming is the stage when the group first comes together. Everybody is very polite and very dull. Conflict is seldom voiced directly, mainly personal and definitely destructive. Since the grouping is new, the individuals will be guarded in their own opinions and generally reserved. This is particularly so in terms of the more nervous and/or subordinate members who may never recover. The group tends to defer to a large extent to those who emerge as leaders.

Storming is the next stage, when all Hell breaks loose and the leaders are lynched. Factions form, personalities clash, noone concedes a single point without first fighting tooth and nail. Most importantly, very little communication occurs since no one is listening and some are still unwilling to talk openly. True, this battle ground may seem a little extreme for the groups to which you belong - but if you look beneath the veil of civility at the seething sarcasm, invective and innuendo, perhaps the picture come more into focus.

Norming. At this stage the sub-groups begin to recognize the merits of working together and the in-fighting subsides. Since a new spirit of co-operation is evident, every member begins to feel secure in expressing their own view points and these are discussed openly with the whole group. The most significant improvement is that people start to listen to each other. Work methods become established and recognized by the group as a whole.

Performing. This is the culmination, when the group has settled on a system which allows free and frank exchange of views and a high degree of support by the group for each other and its own decisions.

In terms of performance, the group starts at a level slightly below the sum of the individuals' levels and then drops abruptly to its nadir until it climbs during Norming to a new level of Performing which is (hopefully) well above the start. It is this elevated level of performance which is the main justification for using the group process rather than a simple group of staff.

5.4 Group Skills

The group process is a series of changes which occur as a group of individuals form into a cohesive and effective operating unit. If the process is understood, it can be accelerated.

There are two main sets of skills which a group must acquire:

1. Managerial Skills
2. Interpersonal Skills.

As a self-managing unit, a group has to undertake most of the functions of a Group Leader - collectively. For instance, meetings must be organized, budgets decided, strategic planning undertaken, goals set, performance monitored, reviews scheduled, etc. It is increasingly recognized that it is a fallacy to expect an individual to suddenly assume managerial responsibility without assistance; in the group it is even more so. Even if there are practiced managers in the group, they must first agree on a method, and then convince and train the remainder of the group.

As a collection of people, a group needs to relearn some basic manners and people-management skills. Again, think of that self-opinionated, cantankerous loud-mouth; he/she should learn good manners, and the group must learn to enforce these manners without destructive confrontation.

5.5 Accelerating Development

It is common practice in accelerating group development

to appoint, and if necessary train, a "group facilitator". The role of this person is to continually draw the groups' attention to the group process and to suggest structures and practices to support and enhance the group skills. This must be only a short-term training strategy, however, since the existence of a single facilitator may prevent the group from assuming collective responsibility for the group process. The aim of any group should be that facilitation is performed by every member equally and constantly. If this responsibility is recognised and undertaken from the beginning by all, then the Storming phase may be avoided and the group development passed straight into Norming.

The following is a set of suggestions which may help in group formation. They are offered as suggestions, no more; a group will work towards its own practices and norms.

Focus

The two basic foci should be the group and the task. If something is to be decided, it is the group that decides it. If there is a problem, the group solves it. If a member is performing badly, it is the group who asks for change.

If individual conflicts arise, review them in terms of the task. If there is initially a lack of structure and purpose in the deliberations, impose both in terms of the task. If there are disputes between alternative courses of action, negotiate in terms of the task.

Clarification

In any group work management, the clarity of the specification is of dominant importance - in group work it is exponentially so. The same reasoning hold for every decision and action taken throughout the life of the group.

It is the first responsibility of the group to clarify its own task, and to record this understanding so that it can be constantly seen. This mission statement may be revised or replaced, but it should always act as a focus for the group's deliberations and actions.

The mouse

In any group, there is always the quiet one in the corner who doesn't say much. That individual is the most underutilized resource in the whole group, and so represents the best return for minimal effort by the group as a whole. It is the responsibility of that individual to speak out and to contribute. It is the responsibility of the group to encourage and develop that person, to include him/ her in the discussion and actions, and to provide positive reinforcement each time that happens.

The loud-mouth

In any group, there is always a dominant member whose opinions form a lopsided share of the discussion. It is the responsibility of each individual to consider whether they are that person. It is the responsibility of the group to ask whether the loud-mouth might like to summarize briefly, and then ask for other views.

The written record

Often a decision which is not recorded will become clouded and have to be re-discussed. This can be avoided simply by recording on a large display (where the group can clearly see) each decision as it is made. This has the further advantage that each decision must be expressed in a clear and concise form which ensures that it is clarified.

Feedback (negative)

All criticism must be neutral: focused on the task and not the personality. It is wise to adopt the policy of giving feedback frequently, especially for small things - this can be couched as mutual coaching, and it reduces the destructive impact of criticism when things go badly wrong. Every criticism must be accompanied by a positive suggestion for improvement.

Feedback (positive)

If anyone does something well, praise it. Not only does this re-enforce commendable actions, but it also mollifies the negative feedback which may come later. Progress in the task should be emphasized.

5.6 Handling Failure

The long term success of a group depends upon how it deals with failure. Tendency to brush off failure and to get on with the next stage with no more than a mention is a very foolish one. Any failure should be explored by the group. This is not to attribute blame (for that is shared by the whole group as an individual only acts with delegated responsibility), but rather to examine the causes and to devise a mechanism which either monitors against or prevents repetition. A mistake should only happen once if it is treated correctly.

One practice which is particularly useful is to delegate the agreed solution to the individual or sub-group who made the original error. This allows the group to demonstrate its continuing trust and the penitent to make amends.

5.7 Handling Deadlock

If two opposing points of view are held in the group then some action must be taken. Several possibly strategies exist. Each sub-group could debate from the other sub-group's view-point in order to better understand it. Common ground could be emphasized, and the differences viewed for a possible middle or alternative strategy. Each could be debated in the light of the original task. But firstly the group should decide how much time the debate actually merits and then guillotine it after that time - then, if the issue is not critical, toss a coin.

Sign posting

As each small point is discussed, the larger picture can be obscured. Thus it is useful frequently to remind the group: this is where we came from, this is where we got to, and this is where we should be going.

Avoid single solutions

First ideas are not always best. For any given problem, the group should generate alternatives, evaluate these in terms of the task, pick one and implement it. But most importantly, they must also monitor the outcome, schedule a review and be prepared to change the plan.

Active communication

Communication is the responsibility of both the speaker and the listener. The speaker must actively seek to express the ideas in a clear and concise manner — the listener must actively seek to understand what has been said and to ask for clarification if unsure. Finally, both parties must be sure that the ideas have been correctly communicated perhaps by the listener summarizing what was said in a different way.

6

Small Group Facilitation

Sivasailam Thiagarajan, Ph.D. and his associates at Thiagi Inc. have identified the "Six Tensions in Small-Group Activities". These can be used to reflect upon when facilitating to the self help groups.

6.1 Structure

How rigidly or flexibly should the small-group activity be implemented?

Tightest : Explain the rules in detail at the beginning and enforce them rigidly.

Tight : Announce the rules in the beginning and enforce them fairly strictly.

Neutral : Give an overview of the rules and enforce them flexibly.

Loose : Explain the rules only when needed and apply them loosely.

Loosest : Make up the rules as you go along and use them arbitrarily.

6.2 Pace

How rapidly or leisurely should the small-group activity be implemented?

Fastest : Constantly rush the participants and impose tight time limits.

Fast : Keep the activity moving at a fairly fast pace.

Neutral : Keep the activity moving at a comfortable pace.

Slow : Keep the activity proceeding at a fairly slow pace.

Slowest : Constantly slow down the activity.

6.3 Interaction

How do group members relate to each other?

Most cooperative : Maintain a high level of cooperation by focusing on external threats and obstacles.

Cooperative : Deemphasize scores and encourage the participants to help each other.

Neutral : Maintain a balance between cooperation and competition

Competitive : Keep scores and encourage participants to outperform their opponents.

Most competitive : Encourage cut-throat competition by constantly pointing out that winning is the only thing, and announce a reward to be given to the winner.

6.4 Focus

Which is more important, a positive procedure or efficient results?

Most process-focused : Keep the activity interesting, playful, and creative.

Process-focused : Keep the activity enjoyable.

Neutral : Maintain a balance between an enjoyable procedure and efficient results.

Results-focused : De-emphasize the enjoyment of the activity and focus on getting the job done.

Most results-focused : Constantly emphasize the goals, results, and outcomes of the activity

6.5 Concern

Are we most concerned about individual or group needs?

Greatest individual concern : Focus on individual needs and ignore group needs.

Individual concern : Focus a little bit more on individual needs than on group needs.

Neutral : Maintain a balance between individual needs and group needs.

Group concern : Focus a little more on group needs than individual needs.

Greatest group concern : Focus on group needs and ignore individual needs.

6.6 Control

Where should group members look for direction and validation?

Most internal : Take an unobtrusive role. Let the group decide what is valuable to them.

Internal : Take a background role. Avoid giving suggestions and feedback.

Neutral : Maintain a balance between participating and withdrawing from group activities.

External : Take a consultant role. Give suggestions and feedback.

Most external : Take a leadership role. Provide authoritative advice and evaluation.

6.7 Maintaining a Balance

The appropriate location of an activity along the six tensions depends on several factors, including the number and type of participants and the structure and purpose of the activity.

The secret of effective facilitation is to make these tensions transparent. This is achieved by maintaining a balance between the two poles of each tension. Unfortunately, however, "balance" resides in the perception of the participants rather than in outside reality. Thus, the balance between cooperation and competition may differ drastically between groups.

6.8 Tactics to Overcome Tensions

The first step in making the tensions transparent is to avoid the extremes. Beyond that, you may use a variety of tactics to increase or decrease the elements in each tension. Here are a couple of sample tactics for each element:

To tighten the structure. . .

Begin with a detailed explanation of the rules of the activity. Stress the importance of adhering to these rules. Provide a printed copy of the rules to each participant. Frequently refer to these rules.

To loosen the structure. . .

Acknowledge that the participants will be initially

confused. Reassure them it is not absolutely necessary to stick to the rules. Don't present all the rules in the beginning. Introduce the rules only if and when they are required.

To speed up the pace...

Begin the activity promptly and get it rolling fast. Announce and implement intermediate time limits.

To slow down the pace...

Announce and implement minimum time requirements. If a participant or a team finishes the task before this time is up, insist on review and revision. Introduce a quality-control rule that punishes participants and teams for turning in sloppy ideas or products.

To increase competition...

Use a scoring system to reward effective performance. Periodically announce and compare the scores of different individuals or teams. Reward the winning team with a valuable prize.

To increase cooperation...

Reduce the conflict among the participants and increase the conflict between the participants and external constraints (for example, time limits). Use multiple criteria for determining the winners: Reward individuals or teams for speed, quality, efficiency, fluency, creativity, novelty, and other such factors.

To increase the focus on the process...

Make the procedure more enjoyable by introducing game elements such as bonus scores and chance. From time to time, stop the procedure and undertake a process check. Let the participants suggest changes for making the procedure more interesting.

To increase the focus on the results...

Use a scoring system to reward efficient performance by individuals or teams. Stop the procedure and discuss the desired results. Have the participants commit themselves to getting the job done.

To pay more attention to individual needs...

If participants are at different levels of skill or knowledge, organize them into teams of approximately equal strength. Encourage timid people to participate more by providing them with additional information and responsibilities.

To pay more attention to group needs...

Identify dominant participants and give them additional roles (for example, keeping score or taking notes) to channel their excess energy. Have the team conduct periodic process checks to make sure everyone's needs are met.

To increase external control...

Turn the lights off to get everyone's attention before making important announcements. Use confederates among the participants and in different teams to ensure external command and control.

To increase internal control...

Explain your role as that of a facilitator rather than those of a leader or an expert. When participants ask you a procedural question (for example, "What should we do next?"), refer it back to the group with a question such as "What would you like to do next?"

6.9 A Procedural Model for Effective Facilitation

A six-step procedural model for using the tension-adjustment tactics before, during, and after group activity authored by management gurus is given below.

Step 1. Identify preferences

Flexible facilitation does not mean that the facilitator should not have personal preferences, but should be aware of these preferences and keep them under control. For example, one may prefer a fairly loose structure, fast pace, cooperative interaction, results focus, individual concern, and external control. It is important to be aware of biases and to realize they may not meet the needs of the group.

The best way to discover biases is to recall small-group experiences which felt very positive or very negative and to analyze the factors that contributed to those feelings. Once aware of the biases, remind to relegate them to the background whenever necessary.

Step 2. Identify participant preferences

Before planning a small-group activity, the facilitator needs to collect information on the likely preferences of the participants along each of tension areas. The best source of information is a representative sample from the group. The best strategy for collecting the information is to interview the participants using the behavioral scale presented earlier.

To cross-check information the facilitator may wish to talk to other facilitators, consultants, and trainers who are familiar with the group.

Step 3. Design or revise the small-group activity to suit participant preferences

Whether designing a new simulation game or using an existing one, integrate the understanding of the participants' preferences into the activity. Carefully work through the steps and rules of the activity to decide where they appear to be located along each tension. For example, if there are several complex rules that are rigid, the activity will be perceived to be too tight by most participants- unless their preference is for a high degree of structure. When tension areas at one extreme or another is identified, use appropriate tactics to make suitable adjustments. During this step, one may want to work with a few members of the participant group and with a few knowledgeable colleagues to ensure that the design adjustments are appropriate.

Step 4. Conduct the small-group activity

With the appropriate initial adjustments, the facilitator should start the activity with confidence. Do not worry about making additional adjustments at this stage. Present an overview of the process and the desired products to get the group started.

Step 5. Make modifications on the fly

As the participants work through the activity, continuously monitor the levels of various tensions. If the six tensions are at optimum levels, do not interfere with the flow of the activity. However, there is no such thing as a perfect small-group activity, and some tensions are likely to become prominent from time to time. Wait a little while to see if the group makes its own adjustments. Most groups, especially experienced ones, work out their own system of reducing the tensions. With inexperienced groups, it may be needed to intervene with appropriate adjustments. Do this as quickly and as unobtrusively as possible. Continue monitoring the group and adjusting the simulation game as required.

Step 6. Debrief the group

Even after the activity is completed, the facilitators still have a critical step to undertake. Conduct a debriefing session with all participants immediately, and with a few selected participants later, to collect information on their perceptions of different tension levels. This can be done in a few minutes by asking the participants questions based on the rating scale such as, "When did you feel the activity was too tightly structured?" or "When did you feel the facilitator interrupted you too often?" Take notes on the participants' responses and use them to balance the same activity with future groups or activities with the same group. The effectiveness of small-group activities depends heavily on the flexibility of the facilitator.

7

Entrepreneurship

7.1 What is meant by Entrepreneurship?

The concept of entrepreneurship was first established in the 1700s, and the meaning has evolved ever since. Many simply equate it with starting one's own business. Most economists believe it is more than that. To some economists, the entrepreneur is one who is willing to bear the risk of a new venture if there is a significant chance for profit. Others emphasize the entrepreneur's role as an innovator who markets his innovation. Still other economists say that entrepreneurs develop new goods or processes that the market demands and are not currently being supplied.

In the 20th century, economist Joseph Schumpeter (1883-1950) focused on how the entrepreneur's drive for innovation and improvement creates upheaval and change. Schumpeter viewed entrepreneurship as a force of "creative destruction." The entrepreneur carries out "new combinations," thereby helping render old industries obsolete. Established ways of doing business are destroyed by the creation of new and better ways to do them.

Business expert Peter Drucker (1909-2005) took this idea further, describing the entrepreneur as someone who actually searches for change, responds to it, and exploits change as an opportunity. A quick look at changes in communications–from typewriters to personal computers to the Internet–illustrates these ideas.

Most economists today agree that entrepreneurship is a necessary ingredient for stimulating economic growth and employment opportunities in all societies. In the developing world, successful small businesses are the primary engines of job creation, income growth, and poverty reduction. Therefore, government support for entrepreneurship is a crucial strategy for economic development.

7.2 Who can become an Entrepreneur?

There is no one definitive profile. Successful entrepreneurs come in various ages, income levels, gender, and race. They differ in education and experience. But research indicates that most successful entrepreneurs share certain personal attributes, including: creativity, dedication, determination, flexibility, leadership, passion, self-confidence, and "smarts."

Creativity is the spark that drives the development of new products or services, or ways to do business. It is the push for innovation and improvement. It is continuous learning, questioning, and thinking outside of prescribed formulas.

Dedication is what motivates the entrepreneur to work hard, 12 hours a day or more, even seven days a week, especially in the beginning, to get the endeavor off the ground. Planning and ideas must be joined by hard work to succeed. Dedication makes it happen.

Determination is the extremely strong desire to achieve success. It includes persistence and the ability to bounce back after rough times. It persuades the entrepreneur to make the 10th phone call, after nine have yielded nothing. For the true entrepreneur, money is not the motivation. Success is the motivator; money is the reward.

Flexibility is the ability to move quickly in response to changing market needs. It is being true to a dream while also being mindful of market realities. A story is told about an entrepreneur who started a fancy shop selling only French pastries. But customers wanted to buy muffins as well. Rather than risking the loss of these customers, the entrepreneur modified her vision to accommodate these needs.

Leadership is the ability to create rules and to set goals. It is the capacity to follow through to see that rules are followed and goals are accomplished.

Passion is what gets entrepreneurs started and keeps them there. It gives entrepreneurs the ability to convince others to believe in their vision. It can't substitute for planning, but it will help them to stay focused and to get others to look at their plans.

Self-confidence comes from thorough planning, which reduces uncertainty and the level of risk. It also comes from expertise. Self-confidence gives the entrepreneur the ability to listen without being easily swayed or intimidated.

Every entrepreneur has these qualities in different degrees. But what if a person lacks one or more? Many skills can be learned. Or, someone can be hired who has strengths that the entrepreneur lacks. The most important strategy is to be aware of strengths and to build on them.

7.3 Profile of an Entrepreneur

What are the characteristics of an entrepreneur? How does an entrepreneur think? Is your personal profile similar to that of a successful entrepreneur?

Until recently, entrepreneurs were not widely studied. There was a general lack of knowledge and information about what made them tick. The recent interest in revitalizing India's dormant productivity has changed all that. Most business universities now offer courses in entrepreneurship. As a result, business professionals have learned a lot about what it takes to become a successful entrepreneur. Although no one has found the perfect entrepreneurial profile, there are many characteristics that show up repeatedly. In the sections that follow, we'll cover several important characteristics of entrepreneurs for you to consider and dispel the entrepreneurial myths.

A series of interviews were conducted with distinguished entrepreneurs. They were asked what characteristics they felt were essential to success as an entrepreneur. Good health was a characteristic mentioned by every entrepreneur interviewed. Entrepreneurs are physically resilient and in good health. They can work for extended periods of time, and while they are in the process of building their business, they refuse to get sick.

In small businesses, where there is no depth of management, the leader must be there. You may not be able to afford a support staff to cover all business functions, and therefore you will need to work long hours. We all know people who use part of their sick leave each year when they are not sick. Entrepreneurs are not found in this group. At the end of the eight-hour day, when everyone else leaves for home, the entrepreneur will often continue to work into the evening, developing new business ideas.

Self-Control

Entrepreneurs do not function well in structured organizations and do not like someone having authority over them. Most believe they can do the job better than anyone else and will strive for maximum responsibility and accountability. They enjoy creating business strategies and thrive on the process of achieving their goals. Once they achieve a goal, they quickly replace it with a greater goal. They strive to exert whatever influence they can over future events.

In large, structured organizations, entrepreneurs are easy to recognize by the statements they make: "If they wanted that job done right, they should have given it to me." A dominant characteristic of entrepreneurs is their belief that they are smarter than their peers and superiors. They have a compelling need to do their own thing in their own way. They need the freedom to choose and to act according to their own perception of what actions will result in success.

Self-Confidence

Entrepreneurs are self-confident when they are in control of what they're doing and working alone. They tackle problems immediately with confidence and are persistent in their pursuit of their objectives. Most are at their best in the face of adversity, since they thrive on their own self-confidence.

Sense of Urgency

Entrepreneurs have a never-ending sense of urgency to develop their ideas. Inactivity makes them impatient, tense, and uneasy. They thrive on activity and are not likely to be found sitting on bank fishing unless the fish are biting. When they are in the entrepreneurial mode, they are more likely to be found getting things done instead of fishing.

Entrepreneurs prefer individual sports, such as golf, skiing, or tennis, over team sports. They prefer games in which their own brawn and brain directly influence the outcome and pace of the game. They have drive and high energy levels, they are achievement-oriented, and they are tireless in the pursuit of their goals.

Comprehensive Awareness

Successful entrepreneurs can comprehend complex

situations that may include planning, making strategic decisions, and working on multiple business ideas simultaneously. They are farsighted and aware of important details, and they will continuously review all possibilities to achieve their business objectives. At the same time, they devote their energy to completing the tasks immediately before them.

Accounting reports illustrate this characteristic. Accountants spend hours balancing the accounts and closing them out. For them, the achievement is to have balanced books. The entrepreneur only wants to know the magnitude of the numbers and their significance for the operation of the business.

Realism

Entrepreneurs accept things as they are and deal with them accordingly. They may or may not be idealistic, but they are seldom unrealistic. They will change their direction when they see that change will improve their prospects for achieving their goals. They want to know the status of a given situation at all times. News interests them if it is timely, and factual, and provides them with information they need. They will verify any information they receive before they use it in making a decision. Entrepreneurs say what they mean and assume that everyone else does too. They tend to be too trusting and may not be sufficiently suspicious in their business dealings with other people.

Conceptual Ability

Entrepreneurs possess the ability to identify relationships quickly in the midst of complex situations. They identify problems and begin working on their solution faster than other people. They are not troubled by ambiguity and uncertainty because they are used to solving problems. Entrepreneurs are natural leaders and are usually the first to identify a problem to be overcome. If it is pointed out to them that their solution to a problem will not work for some valid reason, they will quickly identify an alternative problem-solving approach.

Status Requirements

Entrepreneurs find satisfaction in symbols of success that are external to themselves. They like the business they have built to be praised, but they are often embarrassed by praise directed at them personally. Their egos do not prevent them from seeking facts, data, and guidance. When they need help, they will not hesitate to admit it especially in areas that are outside of their expertise. During tough business periods, entrepreneurs will concentrate their resources and energies on essential business operations. They want to be where the action is and will not stay in the office for extended periods of time.

Symbols of achievement such as position have little relevance to them. Successful entrepreneurs find their satisfaction of status needs in the performance of their business, not in the appearance they present to their peers and to the public. They will postpone acquiring status items like a luxury car until they are certain that their business is stable.

Interpersonal Relationships

Entrepreneurs are more concerned with people's accomplishments than with their feelings. They generally avoid becoming personally involved and will not hesitate to sever relationships that could hinder the progress of their business. During the business-building period, when resources are scarce, they seldom devote time to dealing with satisfying people's feelings beyond what is essential to achieving their goals.

Their lack of sensitivity to people's feelings can cause turmoil and turnover in their organization. Entrepreneurs are impatient and drive themselves and everyone around them. They don't have the tolerance or empathy necessary for team building unless it's their team, and they will delegate very few key decisions.

As the business grows and assumes an organizational structure, entrepreneurs go through a classic management crisis. For many of them, their need for control makes it difficult for them to delegate authority in the way that a structured organization demands. Their strong direct approach induces them to seek information directly from its source, bypassing the structured chains of authority and responsibility. Their moderate interpersonal skills, which were adequate during the start-up phases, will cause them problems as they try to adjust to the structured or corporate organization. Entrepreneurs with good interpersonal skills will be able to adjust and survive as their organization grows and becomes more structured. The rest won't make it.

Emotional Stability

Entrepreneurs have a considerable amount of self-control and can handle business pressures. They are comfortable in stress situations and are challenged rather than discouraged by setbacks or failures. Entrepreneurs are uncomfortable when things are going well. They'll frequently find some new activity on which to vent their pent-up energy. They are not content to leave well enough alone. Entrepreneurs tend to handle people problems with action plans without empathy. Their moderate interpersonal skills are often inadequate to provide for stable relationships. However, the divorce rate among entrepreneurs is about average.

PART TWO
PRACTICAL FACILITATION SKILLS AND TOOLS

8

Creativity Development

Creativity may be defined as "a mental process involving the generation of new ideas or concepts, or new associations of the creative mind between existing ideas or concepts." Creativity is one of the most crucial ingredients of an entrepreneur. It is that attribute of an entrepreneur which makes him/ her stand out among the crowd, distinguishing apart from the common mass.

Creativity is typically used to refer to the act of producing new ideas, approaches or actions, while innovation is the process of both generating and applying such creative ideas in some specific context.

In the context of an organization, therefore, the term innovation is often used to refer to the entire process by which an organization generates creative new ideas and converts them into novel, useful and viable commercial products, services, and business practices, while the term creativity is reserved to apply specifically to the generation of novel ideas by individuals or groups, as a necessary step within the innovation process.

It is an age-old debates whether creativity and innovation is fostered or born with. Even so, several techniques and tools are developed to enhance creativity in a person. A growing number of psychologists are supporting the idea that there are methods of increasing the creativity of an individual. Several different researchers have proposed approaches to prop up this idea, ranging from psychological-cognitive, such as:

- Osborn-Parnes Creative problem solving
- Synectics;
- Inventium and science-based creative thinking
- Purdue Creative Thinking Program;
- Lateral thinking (courtesy of Edward de Bono),
- TRIZ (the Theory of Inventive Problem-Solving);
- ARIZ (the Algorithm of Inventive Problem-Solving), both developed by the Russian scientist Genrich Altshuller; and
- Computer-Aided Morphological analysis.

8.1 Facilitating Creativity

The first task in becoming facilitating creativity is understanding creativity. Therefore, the facilitator must first develop his own creativity level. If the facilitator knows how to enhance his creativity level, he/she will be able to facilitate to the group.

Action Steps

Here are a few additional things you can do to improve creativity development skills:

- Study books on creative thinking techniques and put them into practice
- Attend courses on creative thinking and put the ideas into practice.

- Keep a daily journal and record of thoughts, ideas, sketches, etc. Review the journal regularly and see what ideas can be developed.
- Indulge in relaxation activities and sports to give the mind a rest and time for the subconscious to digest information.
- Develop an interest in a variety of different things, preferably well away from your normal sphere of work. For example, read comic books or magazines. This keeps the brain busy with new things. It is a common trait of creative people that they are interested in a wide variety of subjects.
- Avoid working too hard – take needed time away from a problem to be creative after periods of intense focus.

It really helps to think of creativity as a skill or set of skills. By practicing, one can get better at using them. So whenever given a chance, try and do mundane things in novel ways - it will make them more entertaining and will get more used to expressing abilities. Practicing at overcoming irrational inhibitions will also help to improve creativity. When at a standstill, and you witness somebody with a vital and flowing creative force, it can be intimidating. The thing that's easy to miss when caught up in the magic of somebody doing something effortlessly that seems impossible is that it doesn't happen all at once. Anything can be achieved by breaking it down into its component parts. Creativity requires patience and a willingness to work for a creative outcome rather than simply wait for enlightenment. Still, it is important to creativity to happen. This can be encouraged by setting up an environment that encourages creative output, a comfortable space within which feels non-threatened and able to create. A program to improve personal creativity might include the following steps.

First, set a measurable goal. Some goals might be:

- to generate 10% more solutions within 6 months
- to come up with an original solution for problem "X" within 2 weeks
- to practice generating ideas by brainstorming (for example, "find at least 100 ideas for a new pen")
- to find a new and effective way to relate to my children that results in them wanting to spend more time with me

Second, set up criteria to indicate whether or not you have or are reaching your goal. Typical criteria are:

- the ideas are novel (in that particular context)
- the ideas are useful, they solve the problem or meet the challenge
- the ideas can be implemented within an appropriate time and budget

Third, read and learn about creativity. This information can be gathered from books, conferences, other people, software products and the Internet. Spend time with people who you believe are creative and ask them how they did it. There are many paths to creativity.

Fourth, surround yourself with people who love and respect you; people who encourage you to take risks.

Fifth, celebrate your progress in reaching your creativity goals.

Finally, begin thinking of yourself as a creative person. Surround that identity with beliefs about your creative abilities. Learn the skills of creativity, act creatively every opportunity you get and find environments that support creative behavior.

Creativity is increased by acknowledging that it exists and by nurturing it. Create a sensory stimulating environment, increase awareness of that environment and provide sufficient quiet time to allow that sensory stimulation to be translated into external reality ... a poem, a bridge, a meal, a song, a quilt, a business report, a game, a dance, a garden. Flood yourself with information in your chosen area of creativity, and then deliberately expose yourself to information outside your area. Respect and care for your creativity as you would a child. Attend to your needs, listen to your creative inner voice, and spend time with yourself. Manage stress in your life as much as possible.

Practice relaxing activity such as handwork or quiet exercise. Avoid becoming too entrenched in your routines.

Creativity is not a gift of some sort, it is a state of being ("un etat d'ame", as they say in French). Learning a creativityincreasing technique of some sort will give you some tools and help you, but will not automatically change your point of view about yourself and your creativity; your belief and value systems about creativity and creativity myths must change as well.

8.2 Obstacles to Creativity

Being too busy and getting too involved with a problem, having conflicting goals and objectives, not allowing enough time to relax, Competition in the present environment can hamper motives for creative output. Concerns with job advancement or opportunities as opposed to job stability or security may affect motives to be creative at work. Also, business corporations have found that the creativeness of their employees are promoted when the structure of their organization is less hierarchical and more democratic and free flowing.

The clearest example of environmental influence is when one is creative in virtue of serendipity. These are instances when the environment facilitates creativity by affording stimulating observations. One study suggested that cues in the environment while completing one task can facilitate insight on a later task, without the subject's awareness. Moreover, there have been many historical accounts that claim the Zeitgeist or cohorts at a particular point in time have influenced events.

Most of the obstacles to creativity can be found within self.

- Fear of criticism
- Lack of confidence
- State of mind/body (for example experiencing negative stress).

The main thing that hinders creative thinking is the belief that one is not creative. Look at it this way. If you tell yourself: "I am a creative person", then you have to have beliefs about yourself that support that identity. If you tell yourself, "I am just an ordinary human being", then you will have a different set of beliefs. Once you have a particular identity and set of beliefs about yourself, you will become interested in seeking out the skills needed to express your identity and beliefs. Affirmations can be used to create a suitable self-image. Creativity is hampered by a too-hectic environment that does not provide quiet time for reflection and introspection. It is also hampered by:

- a sterile environment that does not feed the senses
- demands for quick production of results.
- harsh words (from others or from ourselves)
- by rigid rules and barriers that prevent us from gathering information and/or from connecting with others.

Dehumanizing mass media can contribute to limitations on creativity. Spend less time immersed in popular culture (television or listening to pop music), or take conscious breaks from the everyday world to practice creative thinking.

Other factors that limit creative behavior include:

Stress. Stress is not only a distraction which drains energy which could otherwise be used creatively; it is bad for one's health.

Routines. Routines or set ways of performing tasks have their uses, but allowing them to become too entrenched in one's life causes one to limit the range of responses available and can lead to the development of the anathema of creativity, the "bureaucratic mind".

Beliefs. Having a strong belief in something not only limits our response options, but causes us to limit the way in which we perceive and process information from the outside world. We may "filter out" information which contradicts our belief, and end up in our own "reality tunnel", in which we remain blissfully unaware of much that occurs in front of our very eyes.

Ego. Having a strong ego identity with a particular belief exacerbates this situation and can lead to us aggressively defending it, to the detriment of ourselves, our creativity, and society. This is not to imply that one must have no beliefs merely that one needs to be very aware of one's beliefs and consequent limitations.

Fear. Fear of self expression and of the judgment of others can severely limit one's creativity.

Self-criticism. Negative thinking and self criticism are also limiting factors of an individual's creativity.

Here are a few exercises offered by Mind Tools (North America) Ltd. to help the facilitator in nurturing creativity to his group members.

Exercise No. 1

Reversal - *Improving Products and Services*

Reversal is a good tool for improving a product or a service. To use it, ask the opposite of the question you want to ask, and apply the results.

Example

Imagine that you want to improve the response of a service center. Using Reversal you would ask 'How would I **reduce** customer satisfaction?' After considering this question you might give the following answers:

- Not answering the phone when customers call
- Not returning phone calls
- Have people with no product knowledge answering the phone
- Use rude staff
- Give the wrong advice.

After using Reversal, you would ensure that appropriate staff members were handling incoming phone calls efficiently and pleasantly. You would set up training programs to ensure that they were giving accurate and effective advice.

Key Points

Reversal is a good, easy process for improving products and services. It can be used by asking the exact opposite of the question one want answered, and then apply the results appropriately.

Exercise No. 2

SCAMPER - *Generating new products and services*

SCAMPER is a checklist that helps to think of changes that can be made to an existing product to create a new one.

These changes can be used either as direct suggestions or as starting points for lateral thinking.

Developed by Bob Eberle, the changes SCAMPER stands for are:

- S - Substitute - components, materials, people
- C - Combine - mix, combine with other assemblies or services, integrate
- A - Adapt - alter, change function, use part of another element
- M - Modify - increase or reduce in scale, change shape, modify attributes (e.g. colour)
- P - Put to another use
- E - Eliminate - remove elements, simplify, reduce to core functionality
- R - Reverse - turn inside out or upside down, also use of Reversal.

Example

As an example, imagine that you are a manufacturer of nuts and bolts, and you were looking for new products. SCAMPER would give you:

- Substitute - use of high tech materials for niche markets, such as high speed steel? Carbon fiber? Plastics? Glass? Non-reactive material?
- Combine - integrate nut and bolt? Bolt and washer? Bolt and spanner?
- Adapt - put Allen key or Star head on bolt? Countersink head?
- Modify - produce bolts for watches or bridges? Produce different shaped bolts (e.g. screw in plugs)? Pre-painted green bolts?

- Put to another use - bolts as hinge pins? As axles?
- Eliminate - Eliminate nuts, washers, heads, thread, etc.
- Reverse - make dies as well as bolts, make bolts that cut threads for themselves in material, etc.

Using SCAMPER here has helped to define possible new products. Many of the ideas may be impractical or may not suit the equipment used by the manufacturer. However some of these ideas could be good starting points for new products.

Key points

SCAMPER is an acronym for Substitute, Combine, Adapt, Modify, Put to another use, Eliminate, Reverse. This is a list of changes that you could make to existing products and services to open up new opportunities.

Exercise No. 3

DO IT - *A Simple Process for Creativity*

DO IT is a process for creativity. Techniques outlined earlier in this section focus on specific aspects of creative thinking. DO IT bundles them together, and introduces formal methods of problem definition and evaluation. These help you to get the best out of the creativity techniques.

DO IT is an acronym that stands for:

D - Define problem
O - Open mind and apply creative techniques
I - Identify best solution
T - Transform

These stages are explained in more detail below.

How to Use the Tool

1. Define the Problem

This section concentrates on analyzing the problem to

ensure that the correct question is being asked. The following steps will help you to do this:

- Check that you are tackling the problem, not the symptoms of the problem. To do this, ask yourself why the problem exists repeatedly until you get to the root of it.
- Lay out the bounds of the problem. Work out the objectives that you must achieve and the constraints that you are operating under.
- Where a problem appears to be very large, break it down into smaller parts. Keep on going until each part is achievable in its own right, or needs a precisely defined area of research to be carried out. Summarize the problem in as concise a form as possible. Robert W. Olsen suggests that the best way to do this is to write down a number of 2 word problem statements and choose the best one.

2. Open Mind and Apply Creative Techniques

Once you know the problem that you want to solve, you are ready to start generating possible solutions. It is very tempting just to accept the first good idea that you come across. If you do this, you will miss many even better solutions.

At this stage of DO IT we are not interested in evaluating ideas. Instead, we are trying to generate as many different ideas as possible. Even bad ideas may be the seeds of good ones.

You can use the whole battery of creativity techniques covered earlier in this section to search for possible solutions. Each tool has its particular strengths and benefits, depending on the problems that you want to solve. While you are generating solutions, remember that other people will have different perspectives on the problem, and it will almost certainly be worth asking for the opinions of your colleagues as part of this process.

3. Identify the Best Solution

Only at this stage do you select the best of the ideas you have generated. It may be that the best idea is obvious. Alternatively, it may be worth examining and developing a number of ideas in detail before you select one.

When you are selecting a solution, keep in mind your own or your organization's goals. Often decision-making becomes easy once you know these.

4. Transform

Having identified the problem and created a solution to it, the final stage is to implement this solution. This involves not only development of a reliable product from your idea, but all the marketing and business side as well. This may take a great deal of time and energy.

Many very creative people fail at this stage. They will have fun creating new products and services that may be years ahead of what are available on the market. They will then fail to develop them, and watch someone else make a fortune out of the idea several years later.

The first stage in transforming an idea is to develop an Action Plan for the transformation. This may lead to creation of a Business or Marketing Plan. Once you have done this, the work of implementation begins!

DO IT was devised by Robert W Olsen in his book 'The Art of Creative Thinking'.

Key points

DO IT is a structured process for creativity. Using DO IT ensures that you carry out the essential groundwork that helps you to get the most out of creativity tools.

These steps are:

1. Problem Definition: During this stage you apply a number of techniques to ensure that you are asking the right question.
2. Open Mind: Here you apply creativity techniques to generate as many answers as possible to the question you are asking. At this stage you are not evaluating the answers.
3. Identify the best solution: Only at this stage do you select the best solutions from the ones you came up with in step 2. Where you are having difficulty in selecting ideas, use formal techniques to help.
4. Transform: The final stage is to make an Action Plan for the implementation of the solution, and to carry it out. Without implementation, your creativity is sterile.

Exercise No. 4

Applied Imagination – *An Exercise*

(Alex Osborn – 1957)

Put to other uses	**Adapt**	**Modify**
New ways to use as is? Other uses if modified?	What else is like this? What other idea does this suggest? Does the past offer parallel? What could I copy? Whom could I emulate?	New twist? Change meaning, color, motion, sound, odor, form, shape? Other shapes?
Magnify	**Minify**	**Substitute**
What to add? More time? Greater frequency? Stronger? Higher? Longer?	What to subtract? Smaller? Condensed? Miniature? Lower? Shorter?	Who else instead? What else instead? Other ingredient? Other material? Other process?

Thicker? Extra Value? Plus ingredient? Duplicate? Multiply? Exaggerate?	Lighter? Omit? Streamline? Split up? Understate?	Other power? Other place? Other approach? Other tone of voice?
Rearrange	**Reverse**	**Combine**
Interchange components? Other pattern? Other layout? Other sequence? Transpose cause and effect? Change pace? Change schedule?	Transpose positive and negative? How about opposites? Turn it backward? Turn it upside down? Reverse roles? Change shoes? Turn tables? Turn other cheek?	How about a blend, an alloy, an assortment, an ensemble? Combine units? Combine purposes? Combine appeals? Combine ideas?

Exercise No. 5

Shipwrecked!

A group of players are given names of prominent persons and are placed in a scenario where all of them are in a ship about to sink. Since there is only one lifejacket available, each personalities shall give a speech (say 5 minutes) to persuade the judge why he is the right choice to be the sole survivor.

Exercise No. 6

Provocation

Provocations give us original starting points for creative thinking. It is one of the lateral thinking techniques to start off new and novel ideas. Bizarre and outrageous statements are made. The essence lies in exploring all the dimensional possibilities around that shocking statement.

As an example, we could make a statement that 'Houses should not have roofs'. Normally this would not be a good idea! However this leads one to think of houses with opening roofs, or houses with glass roofs. These would allow you to lie in bed and look up at the stars. Once you have made the Provocation, it can use it in a number of different ways, by examining:

- The consequences of the statement
- What the benefits would be
- What special circumstances would make it a sensible solution
- The principles needed to support it and make it work
- How it would work moment-to-moment
- What would happen if a sequence of events was changed
- Etc..

8.3 Tips to Develop Creativity

1. Always carry a small notebook and a pen or pencil around with you. That way, if you are struck by an idea, you can quickly note it down. Upon rereading your notes, you may discover about 90% of your ideas are daft. Don't worry, that's normal. What's important are the 10% that are brilliant.
2. If you're stuck for an idea, open a dictionary, randomly select a word and then try to formulate ideas incorporating this word. You'd be surprised how well this works. The concept is based on a simple but little known truth: freedom inhibits creativity. There are nothing like restrictions to get you thinking.
3. Define your problem. Grab a sheet of paper, electronic notebook, computer or whatever you use to make notes, and define your problem in detail. Read as much as you can about everything possible. Books exercise your brain, provide inspiration and fill you with information that allows you to make creative connections easily.

9

Facilitating Group Development

Thanks to the information resources sites, useful games and exercises to build strong group dynamics are listed below

Exercise No. 1

Team Building Ice Breakers

Team-building ice breakers are used to bring together individuals who are in the early stages of team building. This can help the people start working together more cohesively towards shared goals or plans.

The Human Web

This ice breaker focuses on how people in the group interrelate and depend on each other.

The facilitator begins with a ball of yarn. Keeping one end, pass the ball to one of the participants, and the person to introduce him- or her-self and their role in the organization. Once this person has made their introduction, ask him or her to pass the ball of yarn on to another person in the group. The person handing over the ball must describe how he/she rélates (or expects to relate) to the other person. The process continues until everyone is introduced. To emphasis the interdependencies amongst the team, the facilitator then pulls on the starting thread and everyone's hand should move.

Ball Challenge

This exercise creates a simple, timed challenge for the team to help focus on shared goals, and also encourages people to include other people.

The facilitator arranges the group in a circle and asks each person to throw the ball across the circle, first announcing his or her own name, and then announcing the name of the person to whom they are throwing the ball (the first few times, each person throws the ball to someone whose name they already know.) When every person in the group has thrown the ball at least once, it's time to set the challenge – to pass the ball around all group members as quickly as possible. Time the process, then ask the group to beat that timing. As the challenge progresses, the team will improve their process, for example by standing closer together. And so the group will learn to work as a team.

Hope, Fears and Expectations

Best done when participants already have a good understanding of their challenge as a team. Group people into 2s or 3s, and ask people to discuss their expectations for the event or work ahead, then what they fears and their hopes. Gather the group's response by collating 3-4 hopes, fears and expectation from pairing or threesome.

Word Association

This ice breaker helps people explore the breadth of the area under discussion. Generate a list of words related to the topic of your event or training. For example, in a health and safety workshop, ask participants what words or phrases come to mind relating to "hazardous materials". Participants may suggest: 'danger,' 'corrosive,' 'flammable,' 'warning,' 'skull and crossbones,' etc. Write all suggestions on the board, perhaps clustering by theme. You can use this opportunity to introduce essential terms and discuss the scope (what's in and what's out) of your training or event.

Burning questions

This ice breaker gives each person the opportunity to ask key questions they hope to cover in the event or training. Again you can use this opportunity to discuss key terminology and scope. Be sure to keep the questions and refer back to them as the event progresses and concludes.

Exercise No. 2

Team Role Playing

Team role playing is an excellent exercise for...

- analysing problems from various perspectives
- implementing brainstorming methodology in simulations of real cases
- trying various solutions in a case scenario
- developing team-work, co-operation and creative problem solving in groups
- exercising creative techniques in a risk-free environment

How it works

Role playing is when a group of people act out roles for a particular scenario. For instance, you might train sales people by having two people act out a sale-scenario. One acts as the sales person. The other acts as the customer. This allows trainee sales people to practice their sales techniques. The facilitator and/or other trainees may watch the role play and critique it afterwards.

Team role-playing is similar, except that two or more teams actively participate. For instance, a group of 10 people and facilitator are divided into two teams of five each. One person in each group acts out the relevant role in the scenario. The other four act as coaches providing advice to their actor. The trainer does not take part in either group. Rather she oversees the exercise. To make team role playing more effective, a secret conflict is introduced from the beginning. Only the facilitator is aware of the conflict. Upon completion of the role playing, the facilitator leads a discussion on the role-play.

Exercise No. 3

Building Blocks

(Arya Kumar, Chief - Entrepreneurship Development & IPR Unit, BITS, Pilani)

Introduction

This is a Team Building Exercise that involves every member in the participant teams.

Instructor has 50 wooden cubes to be used by a team to build a tower that should be as high as possible. In the course of adhering to the rules of the game, the team is required to exhibit their team spirit.

Rules of the Game

1. Each team is to build a tower consisting of wooden blocks one above the other.
2. Each block cost Rs 1000
3. In case team builds a tower with 1- 5 blocks, they get Rs 1000 per block.
4. In case team builds a tower with 6 - 10 blocks, they get additional Rs 3000 per block for 6th -10th block used.

5. In case team builds a tower with 11 – 15 blocks, they get Rs. 5000 additional per block for 11th -15th block
6. In case team builds a tower with 16 – 20 blocks, they get Rs 10000 additional per block for 16th to 20th block.
7. In case team builds a tower with 21st and above number of blocks, they get Rs 20000 additional per block.
8. In case tower breaks, they lose all the investment made.
9. For the unused blocks, cost is to be deducted from the earnings made by successfully constructing a tower having X number of blocks with Y amount of value.

The Game

Step 1

Inviting two teams to be formed having 5 members each

Step 2

Each team to spend 5-7 minutes to identify a Leader, Worker– who will be performing the task of building a tower blind folded. He only can touch the blocks, 3 team members (Helper) who can help by communicating but are not suppose to touch the blocks.

Each team is to decide about how many blocks they would like to buy. Each block cost Rs 1000.

Step 3

Do a toss to decide which team would perform the task first.

Step 4

Allow Teams to work:

All other participants to minutely watch the proceedings comments used, verbal and non verbal communications made by team members; how all these facilitate or obstruct the performance of the task. In case team has completed the task by fully utilizing the first lot of blocks bought, instructor would ask the team whether they would like to buy some more blocks, if so, how many? It is important to note how decision was arrived at. Further in case leader and team members have reservation to buy more blocks, a specific question can be posed to the worker to find out, if he is interested in buying few more blocks. If he agrees to buy, how many? It is important to make a note about the process and reaction of various team members. If thought appropriate instructor can also give an opportunity to perform further task by keeping their eyes open.

Same task is to be performed by the other team and details have to be noted.

Conclusion

Facilitator to initiate the discussion by posing various questions to each team such as:

- How target was arrived at?
- Mechanism used to select Leader, Worker and Helpers by each team.
- Feelings and thoughts of the worker and leader while performing the task.
- Reaction of worker, as t o the help he got from his team members. Did he receive clear instructions or confusing instructions? How did it affect the task?
- Reaction of audiences to the performance of both the teams. What went wrong and what was appreciable in both the teams.
- Finally, analyze and consolidate the points that help in building an Effective Team.

Tool No. 1

Group Leadership Motivation Level Analysis

The important factor behind group motivation is the leader. But then, who will motivate the group leader? Motivation may be either or both external or internal. That is why it is helpful for the group to have a highly motivated group leader. The following questionnaire is derived by Mindtools Company, a net-based consultancy and resource centre to analyse the leadership motivation quality. As a facilitator, this tool will provide an effective study on whether the group leader needs to be replaced or initiated further.

Sl.	*Question*	*1*	*2*	*3*	*4*	*5*
1	I am energized when people count on me for ideas.					
2	As a practice, I ask people challenging questions when we are working on projects together.					
3	I take delight in complimenting people that I work with when progress is made.					
4	I find it easy to be the cheerleader for others, when times are good and when times are bad.					
5	Team accomplishment is more important to me than my own personal accomplishments.					
6	People often take my ideas and run with them.					
7	When involved in group projects, building team cohesiveness is important to me.					
8	When involved in group projects,					

(Contd...)

Sl.	*Question*	*1*	*2*	*3*	*4*	*5*
	coaching others is an activity that I gravitate toward.					
9	I find pleasure in recognizing and celebrating the accomplishments of others.					
10	When involved in group projects, my team members' problems are my problems.					
11	Resolving interpersonal conflict is an activity that I enjoy.					
12	When involved in group projects, I frequently find myself to be an "idea generator."					
13	When involved in group projects, I am inclined to let my ideas be known.					
14	I find pleasure in being a convincing person.					
	TOTAL					

Score	*Comment*
14 – 27	This implies a low motivation to lead
28 - 55	This implies some uncertainty over your motivation to lead
56 - 70	This implies a strong motivation to lead.

Tool No. 2

Group Leadership Skill Analysis

The following analysis is again derived from Mindtools and can be advocated to the leader of the micro enterprise. Set the stage for an interview with the facilitated group and ask the following questions and give values according to the magnitude. This is a very comprehensive questionnaire and can be used to diagnose the motivating skill of the group leader. A series of implicational issues are given below to utilize this tool as a remedial counsel by the facilitator. Again, please note that the questions are to be advocated to the group leaders to analyse and diagnose their motivational skills.

Sl.	*Question*	*1*	*2*	*3*	*4*	*5*
1	When faced with a performance problem, I take care to establish whether it is caused by lack of resource, lack of motivation, or lack of skills.					
2	I establish clear performance standards and expectations					
3	The rewards and discipline I use are clearly linked to performance and defined behavioral objectives.					
4	I structure work so that is interesting and challenging, and allows for appropriate autonomy.					
5	When I give a reward I make sure it is one that the recipient values.					
6	I am consistent in the way that I discipline people for substandard performance.					
7	When I see good work, I praise it immediately.					
8	I make sure people have the tools, resources, and training to achieve the results I expect.					
9	I try to understand what motivates each individual member of my team.					

(Contd...)

Sl.	*Question*	*1*	*2*	*3*	*4*	*5*
10	I make a major effort to ensure that I offer competitive wages and other forms of compensation.					
11	In order to be fair, I use the same rewards for everyone when recognizing good performance.					
12	I help people establish performance goals that are challenging and specific, and that are linked to organizational objectives.					
13	I make sure I know what is going on in the real work environment before taking any remedial or disciplinary action.					
14	I encourage people to set their goals high, and make their achievement measurements challenge them fairly.					
15	I try to combine and rotate job assignments so that people can learn and use a variety of skills.					
	TOTAL					

Score Comment to be made to the Group Leader

15 - 34 A great opportunity to improve the way you motivate others, and your and your team's long term success! However, to do this, you've got to fundamentally improve your motivation skills.

35 - 52 Good at some aspects of motivating others, but there's room for improvement elsewhere. Focus on the implication issues below, and most likely you will find that your team's performance will increase.

53 - 75 You're probably motivating your team very effectively! Still, check the implications below to see if there's anything you can use to make this even better.

Implications of the above tool

Providing Productive and Challenging Work (Questions 1, 4, 15)

The first step in building a highly motivated team is providing interesting work, which is well organized to meet the needs and desires of team members. No matter how self-motivated a person is, how challenging the goals he or she sets, or how wonderful the rewards, if the work is badly designed, it will be hard to motivate people and work will be less than ideal.

Effective motivators understand that work design has a strong impact on performance. When a person finds a job inherently unsatisfying, there's not much you can do to motivate him or her. Job design and enrichment combine to match characteristics of the job with workers' skills and interests: The more variety, challenge and autonomy there is to a job, the more intrinsically satisfying it will be.

Setting Effective Goals (Questions 2, 3, 12, 14)

When you are confident that the work you provide is well organized, the next thing to do is to ensure that workers have clear and attainable goals that they're working to achieve. Managing the goal setting process is essential for creating a highly motivating environment. The effectiveness of goal setting in motivation is a well-recognized fact, and by making goals specific, consistent, and appropriately challenging, you can set goals that are powerfully motivating. As such, the SMART (Specific, Measurable, Attainable, Relevant, Time-bound) acronym helps you define effective goals.

Specific goals are measurable, unambiguous and behaviorchanging. They outline exactly what needs to be accomplished, and when it will be considered as "achieved". Having goals that are consistent with other personal goals as well as organizational goals is also important. If goals are inconsistent, the resulting confusion and incompatibility would like cause the person to do nothing rather than work in different directions.

Finally, challenge is important, due to the observation that we get what we expect. Up to a point, the more you expect from someone, the harder they will generally work. This has been shown time and again, and is explained by the idea of Expectancy Theory: The idea here is that you need to link high effort with high performance, and high performance with a positive outcome. With those two linkages established, people are motivated to work hard to achieve a positive outcome.

Understanding Individual Differences in Motivation (Questions 5, 9, 10, 11)

Motivational techniques should bring out the best in people. That means they should build on an individual's strengths and minimize his or her weaknesses.

There are certainly some common denominators in motivation, like fair wages, decent working conditions, a sense of camaraderie with co-workers, and a good relationship with one's supervisor. Abraham Maslow and Frederick Herzberg are two famous motivation theorists who established that even if these sorts of things are not necessarily motivating in themselves, they have to be present in order to even think about enhancing motivation.

However, the assumption in most modern workplaces is that these lower order, "hygiene" factors are being met, and that people are seeking the things that provide real motivation. These are things like challenging work, control, growth opportunities, and recognition for a job well done.

To decide which motivating factors to provide you need to look at the individual employees. Some will be motivated by more time off, while others may prefer to gain status and recognition in the company. Understanding these individual needs is mandatory for building a motivating workplace, and is why question 11 above is a "trick question": if you try to motivate everyone in exactly the same way, you're likely missing plenty of opportunities for motivating individual members of your team.

Providing Rewards and Recognition (Questions 6, 7, 8, 13)

When you know what you want to provide in terms of reward and recognition, it's important to establish an effective system. The primary focus of a reward system is fairness. Both reward and discipline have to be perceived as fairly distributed according to clear guidelines. This is why setting specific performance expectations is so important. ("Fairness" doesn't mean that everyone has the same reward package - it means that differences between people's reward packages need to be clear and understandable.)

It is equally important to make sure you give your team members the tools they need to be successful. If you're setting goals, then you need to make sure that they are attainable, and you do that by providing the necessary support, tools, resources, and training.

It's also important that you get to understand the challenges your team faces. This way you can appreciate the small victories that lead to the major accomplishments. Motivation is all about encouragement and appreciation.

When you are part of the team and not simply an "observer from above" you will have many opportunities to thank people and recognize good work right on the spot. This is a really important factor in successful recognition. You have to be in a position to show or tell people every day that you appreciate their contributions.

10

Identifying Entrepreneurs

The following questionnaire can be administered by the facilitator to the members of the groups to identify the person with the highest entrepreneurial traits. It should be noted that the questionnaire is based on psychological testing to analyze the motivation and attitude level of the person.

The scoring will be done in a 4 point scale in the following format-

Tool No. 1

Entrepreneurial Trait Analysis

To what degree do the statements below correspond to you?

1 Totally disagree 2 Somewhat disagree,

3 Somewhat agree 4 Totally agree

No.	*Variable*	*Score*
1	I am always convinced that my contribution is essential to a project's success	
2	I cannot take action without having all the available information	

(Contd...)

No.	*Variable*	*Score*
3	I like to create challenges for myself when I take on a new project	
4	I am fairly at ease when faced with complex situations	
5	I see opportunities where others see only problems	
6	I like to make my own decisions	
7	Becoming rich is one of my major life goals	
8	The results I obtain depend on my skills and efforts	
9	One must act quickly to take advantage of opportunities	
10	There is not much to be learnt from failure	
11	I do not consider myself more ambitious than others	
12	I am relatively curious, and always trying to discover new things	
13	I am much less efficient in stressful circumstances	
14	Personal satisfaction is more important to me than having a lot of money	
15	When I want something, I always follow through to the end	
16	I find it easy to adhere to the objectives that have been set for me	
17	I want to create something that will be recognized	
18	I look for alternative solutions to difficult problems	
19	One can learn more from one's failures than from one's successes	
20	Success can lead to complacency	
21	I feel that one can have some control over one's fate	
22	I can imagine how things should be done or should work	
23	When I take on a project, I am confident of succeeding	
24	I aim for excellence in all that I do	
25	When embarking on an adventure, failure is a possibility that has to be accepted	
26	I abandon projects when I am not successful	
27	Taking risks prevents me from sleeping at night	

(Contd...)

No.	*Variable*	*Score*
28	When making an important decision, I like to rely on facts rather than my intuition or "gut" feeling	
29	I believe that "luck" is partially of our own making	
30	I am generally wary of my instincts	
31	I do not like to compete with others	
32	I make an effort to be first, or the best, in my area of expertise	
33	I feel that taking risks is like buying lottery tickets - it all boils down to luck	
34	I prefer to be the one making the final decision	
35	I always try to learn something from my failures	
36	I find it easy to identify good opportunities	
37	I enjoy making money more than I do spending it	
38	In my opinion, anything is possible as long as I believe that I can do it	
39	Success is mostly a matter of luck	
40	I do not try to share my personal risks with others	
41	I need rapid feedback on the results of my initiatives	
42	I dislike taking on a project only to prove that I can do it	
43	Stress, to a certain point, spurs me on	
44	I find it easy to motivate others to work with me	
45	Making my dreams come true makes me proud	
46	No matter what one does, one cannot control events	
47	I always try to take calculated risks	
48	I always look for situations where there are several options available	
49	I tend to carefully think over new projects before deciding to move forth with them	
50	I often find that complex situations stop me from taking action	
51	I am able to imagine several solutions to a problem	
52	Nowadays, power is measured by a person's assets	
53	I can easily conceive of several ways of meeting a particular need	

(Contd...)

No.	*Variable*	*Score*
54	I rarely change my mind once it's made up	
55	After a setback, I am able to pick myself up and start over	
56	I appreciate having my successes publicly acknowledged	
57	I do not always feel like making sacrifices to succeed	
58	Fear of failure often stops me from taking on new projects	
59	I do not like influencing others	
60	In order to be satisfied with my achievements, I take on easy projects	
61	When I start a project, I am not always convinced of my ability to successfully complete it	
62	I like to be a leader	
63	I find it difficult to function in uncertain or ambiguous situations	
64	I have a rather good opinion of myself	
65	I do not take risks just for the fun of it	
66	I am always embarking on new projects	
67	Action, and being on the move, are important to me	
68	I have a hard time anticipating events and trends	
69	I hate being the focus of special attention	
70	I want to become an expert in my field	
71	I prefer to keep working by the same old proven methods	
72	I like situations where there are rules to follow	
73	I have been told that I have good timing	
74	Today, one cannot do much with only a limited amount of money	
75	In my opinion, anything is possible as long as I believe I can do it	
76	I tend to put off difficult tasks	
77	I rely heavily on my experience when making important decisions	
78	I tend to see the proverbial glass as "half empty" rather than "half full"	

(Contd...)

No.	*Variable*	*Score*
79	Being overly ambitious is often negatively perceived	
80	I am not motivated by peer recognition	
81	I am not overly interested in becoming renowned in my industry	
82	While there is a time for reflection, there is also – more importantly – a time for action	
83	I am not afraid of showing initiative	
84	I have no problem working for someone else	
85	I prefer to be my own boss	
86	Before making an important move, I always worry about what others will think	
87	I always give my all to anything I do	
88	In ambiguous or uncertain situations, I do a good job of handling any stress I may be experiencing	
89	People make mistakes because they rely overly on their intuition	
90	I feel that money is a good indication of my performance	

Score

Between 150 and 210: Your profile is closer to that of the general population.

Between 240 and 360: Your profile is more characteristic of that of entrepreneurs.

11

Facilitating Business Ideas Sourcing and Idea Generation

According to Dr Gayatri Saberwal, Faculty Scientist, Institute of Bioinformatics and Applied Biotechnology (IBAB), Bangalore: India, the break-ups of existing entrepreneurs in respect of their opportunity identified are:

Enhancement

It implies to the improvement of existing products. For example- from ordinary television to flat screen; from desktop computers to laptops etc.

Extension

Extension refers to the adding utility to an existing product. For example- Mobile handset with camera, FM radio, MP3 player; pen with torchlight etc.

Specialization

Specialization focuses on a particular attribute of an existing product. For example- Low cost airlines like Air Deccan; emergence of speciality clinics etc.

It is interesting to note that only 3-4% of the existing entrepreneurs invested on *truly novel, new and innovative ideas.* The remaining 96% are constituted by enhancements, extensions and specializations.

Business ideas usually fit into one of four categories that were described by H. Igor Ansoff in the Harvard Business Review in 1957:

An existing good or service for an existing market

This is a difficult approach for a start-up operation. It means winning over consumers through merchandising appeal, advertising, etc. Entry costs are high, and profit is uncertain.

A new good or service for a new market

This is the riskiest strategy for a new firm because both the product and the market are unknown. It requires the most research and planning. If successful, however, it has the most potential for new business and can be extremely profitable.

A new good or service for an existing market. (Often this is expanded to include modified goods/services.)

For example, entrepreneurial greeting-card makers use edgy humor and types of messages not produced by Hallmark or American Greetings – the major greeting-card makers – to compete in an existing market.

An existing good or service for a new market

The new market could be a different country, region, or market niche. Entrepreneurs who provide goods/services at customers' homes or offices, or who sell them on the Internet, are also targeting a new market – people who don't like shopping or are too busy to do so.

Finding the Real Opportunities
Business ideas are all around you

They are lurking in your garage, in your basement, in your kitchen, and in your children's room. You'll find them in magazine ads, at your neighbor's house, and at work. They are right there in the vegetables you brought in from the yard . . . in the stack of papers next to your laser printer . . . in the back of your truck . . . and at the back of your mind.

You don't need to be a genius or an MBA to spot those ideas and turn them into profits, either. Identifying business opportunities is often as easy as identifying problems many people share and finding a way to solve them. When Matthew Osborne, an entrepreneur from Columbus, Ohio, wanted a way to make money, he found one right at his feet: dog dirt. Unlike most people who just gripe about stepping in it or having to clean it up, he started a business removing dog waste from homeowners' yards. The business was an immediate success, and after several years, he sold the business for a quarter of a million dollars. Even then, however, he continued to make money from his idea by writing a booklet about how to start a pet waste-removal business and selling the booklet on the Internet.

Other business owners have turned their hobbies, interests, and skills into satisfying and often lucrative businesses, simply by seeing a need in the world around them and finding a way to fill it. You can, too.

Do What You Love to Do Businesses don't just happen. They are made.

Whether you plan to profit by twisting balloons into smile-generating shapes or orchestrating the growth of multimillion-dollar, multinational companies, your success relies on what you bring to the business. If you love what you do, your passion for the business will drive you to be knowledgeable, creative, and persistent. On the other hand, if your feeling for what you do is lukewarm, your success will be, too.

Turn Old Standbys into New ProductsTruly new concepts are few and far between. Most new products or new business ideas are simply spin-offs of old ones. In-line skates are one good example. Essentially, they are ice skates on wheels or, depending on your point of view, streamlined roller-skates. Other new business ideas are nothing more than new ways of marketing mundane products. Take Dial-A-Mattress, for example. Furniture and bedding stores have always sold mattresses—but not by phone. Not until furniture salesman by the name of Napoleon Barragan started a business selling mattresses over an 800-number phone line. The idea took hold, and today, Dial-AMattress sells some $70 million worth of mattresses each year.

You may not have the money, management ability, contacts, or desire to launch a major new product like inline skates or the energy or desire to build a multimillion-dollar sales organization. But you don't have to launch anything that large to start a business or introduce a new product.

Years ago when my kids were little, I made money selling beanbags. The twist? I designed them in the shape of frogs and I filled them with birdseed instead of beans to make them pliable and less lumpy to the touch. To attract attention at craft shows, I displayed them in various human poses (sitting up, laying on their side resting their head on their hand, or hugging each other, for instance). I could produce them quickly and kept my costs low by making the frogs from inexpensive fabric remnants. That allowed me to price the frogs low enough to make them great impulse buys.

You can spin almost any skill or industry knowledge into marketable new products or services.

A neighbour turned his skill at fixing cars into a repair and tune-up service. His angle? He was mobile. Customers didn't have to drop their car off at the shop. Instead, the "shop" (a van outfitted with tools and auto parts) came to them. Another acquaintance built a business by purchasing large quantities of chemicals and repackaging them in smaller quantities.

> And several paper suppliers have created businesses by preprinting colorful brochure or flier designs on paper stock. The preprinted papers are then sold to businesses and individuals who use their laser printers to print out their own sales literature and fliers on an as-needed basis.
>
> The business you start today may not be the business you run tomorrow. Entrepreneurs and self-employed individuals sometimes find that their initial attempts to start a business don't bring in the profits they had hoped for. Nevertheless, they often benefit by discovering new profit-making opportunities because of contacts or knowledge they pick up running their first business.
>
> [Source: http://www.businesstown.com/businessopps/newbiz-realopp.asp]

The facilitator will have to help the group in identifying business opportunities. The group will have to be motivated to contribute ideas, generate possible opportunities under their own initiatives.

Therefore the first step will be organizing brainstorming.

Tool 1

Brainstorming

Theme- Business idea/opportunity

1. Arrange the meeting for a group of the right size and makeup (typically 4-8 people)
2. Write the initial topic on a flipboard, whiteboard or other system where everyone can see it. The better defined, and more clearly stated the problem, the better the session tends to be.
3. Make sure that everyone understands the problem or issue

4. Review the ground rules

- Avoid criticising ideas / suspend judgement. All ideas are as valid as each other
- Lots, Lots & Lots - a large number of ideas is the aim, if you limit the number of ideas people will start to judge the ideas and only put in their 'best' or more often than not, the least radical and new.
- Free-wheeling. Don't censor any ideas, keep the meeting flow going.
- Listen to other ideas, and try to piggy back on them to other ideas.
- Avoid any discussion of ideas or questions, as these stop the flow of ideas.

5. Have someone facilitating to enforce the rules and write down all the ideas as they occur (the scribe can be a second person)
6. Generate ideas - either in an unstructured way (anyone can say an idea at any time) or structure (going round the table, allowing people to pass if they have no new ideas).
7. Clarify and conclude the session. Ideas that are identical can be combined, all others should be kept. It is useful to get a consensus of which ideas should be looked at further or what the next action and timescale is.

Walkman- A case

Walkman is a popular Sony brand used to market its portable audio and video players. The original Walkman introduced a change in music listening habits, allowing people to carry their own choice of music with them. The original Walkman was marketed in the 80s as the Walkman in Japan, the

> Soundabout in many other countries including the US, Freestyle in Sweden and the Stowaway in the UK. The device was created by audio division engineer Nobutoshi Kihara for Sony cochairman Morita, who wanted to be able to listen to operas during his frequent transpacific plane trips. Thus, from a problem, a successful product took birth.

After the brainstorming session is executed, the group will have to have at least 10-15 business ideas with them. It should be noted again that all ideas contributed by every members will have to be presented.

Tool 2

Ideas from a Newspaper

The newspaper exercise is useful for a wide range of audiences, including people just starting to think about entrepreneurship.

We think that this may also be a good exercise to run in a "stand alone" situation: not part of a workshop or course, as it doesn't require any other knowledge of entrepreneurship.

Participant Briefing

a. Providing Context

It is good to give some context to the participants, so that they can appreciate the value of this rather simple exercise, but not to go into the details of the learning objectives, as those should be drawn out in discussion after the exercise.

1) Mention that this exercise starts at the beginning of the company building process – and emphasizes a skill that is often overlooked: idea generation.

2) You may want to outline for them how idea generation leads to opportunity evaluation, and then onward to identifying and recruiting resources, etc.

3) It's important to emphasize that idea generation is required throughout the entrepreneurial process – and in fact is a critical skill when working within organizations, or in many other contexts.

b. Describing exercise

1) Explain to the participants that you will be splitting them into teams of 3 – 5 people, depending on class size. It's good to have at least 4 teams.

2) Explain clearly what you will be asking them to do. (see "Running the Exercise", below.)

Running the Exercise

The Longest List Wins!

1. Have the teams form by counting off into groups of 3 – 5 people. (This exercise works best with at least 4 teams.)

2. Hand each group a section of a recent newspaper (8 pages or so)

3. Ask the teams to come up with as many different ideas for possible businesses as they can in 15 minutes. The ideas must be triggered by something (anything) they see in their section of newspaper.

4. After 15 minutes, each team tells the group how many ideas they generated, and reads off the list to the room. No sorting or preference required. (This is not yet about opportunity identification)

5. While they are reading off their list, you (the facilitator) write each idea on the board. While writing each idea, you group the ideas into three groups, but don't not explain what the groups are (no headers, etc on the board). The ideas should be divided along the following lines:

- Ideas created by consumer taste/spending change

- Those triggered by regulatory change
- And those created by changes in technology Clearly some ideas will fall into more than one category, but try to choose the one that most makes sense, or is at the root of the idea.

6. Lead the participants through a discussion. Some thoughts for discussion triggers and points to draw out:

- You may want to choose a few ideas from the different lists, and ask the teams to explain how they got the idea.
- May want to draw out the similarities and differences in the ideas.
- Can then ask people what the differently grouped ideas have in common with each other.
- Highlight the significance of change making ideas possible.
- Point out where ideas were triggered by "problems" as well.
- Ask why we used a newspaper, in order to highlight need to focus externally.

Note: Discussion should be lively and fun. No idea is silly. No idea is impossible. The same rules apply as for brainstorming!

Tool 3

Idea Card Method

Each person, using Post-it notes or small cards, writes down ideas, and places them next to the person on his or her right. Each person draws a card from there neighbours pile as needed for inspiration. Once the idea has been used, it is passed on to the person on the right along with any new, variations or piggybacked ideas.

연세

12

Facilitating Idea Selection

Tool No. 1

5Qs Analysis

In the previous chapter, we have seen how to generate business ideas and opportunities. The critical part comes when we are to select an idea to bank on. The following questions will have to be used as a primer to select the most appropriate opportunity. The 5Qs are-

1. What important customer problem can you solve?
2. How are you going to do it?
3. How many customers are there those are willing to buy from you?
4. Why can only you provide the solution?
5. How can you defend against competitors?

Ask these questions BEFORE somebody else does! The most important issue regarding the 5Qs is that the group should convince themselves.

Are Chinese restaurants a good opportunity?

Consider two different individuals, each of whom has

the idea to start a chain of mid-priced Chinese food restaurants. They each do some research and find that the market seems large - lots of people are eager to dine out on Chinese food; customers are looking for family fun dining at a reasonable price; there's no competition at that price range or in key locations. All in all, things look promising, each entrepreneur concludes.

Now let's look at their backgrounds: one has been working at high-end Chinese food restaurants in operations for the past 10 years, moving up through junior positions to managing operations for several restaurants. The restaurants have been successful. She is well-liked and respected, and her network comprises chefs, wait staff, operations and marketing people, and suppliers. In addition, she is passionate about food and loves the industry.

The other entrepreneur is a successful investment banker who has analyzed the opportunity based on market trends and has determined that it is interesting. He has no background in hospitality, and no particular passion for food.

Both have the same idea - mid-priced family-oriented Chinese food restaurants. Both have analyzed the markets, customers, industry and competition and have concluded that the idea may be an opportunity. But is it an equally good opportunity for both? Does the restaurateur have a higher chance of success than the banker?

Might the banker have a better chance of success if the idea were to start a financial services business, rather than a restaurant business?

It's clear that the entrepreneur is, in fact, part and parcel of the opportunity. Which explains why we hear venture capitalists talk about "team, team, team" when they do their own analyses. The idea, without the right entrepreneur, remains simply an idea, and does not become an opportunity.

Role of the facilitator

The facilitator will put forward the 5Qs before the groups and note down their discussions.

Reject those ideas which fail at the test of the 5Qs.

Tool No 2

5 Inputs Analysis

List out the '5Q qualified' ideas and analyse each using the 5 Inputs of entrepreneurship. In selecting a project, the facilitator must first understand the implications and importance of five entrepreneurial inputs, namely- Capital, Raw Material, Labour, Skill and Plant.

Capital

Capital is the life-blood of every business concern. Capital is the money you personally have invested in the business and is an indication of how much you have at risk should the business fail. The facilitator must be able to advice the group on how to procure it. Banks, especially, SIDBI and other developmental banks offer loans and aid to the entrepreneurs.

Raw Material

A good that has not been transformed by production; a primary product. A raw material is something that is acted upon by human labour or industry to create some product that human's desire. Often the term is used to denote material that came from nature and is still in an unprocessed or minimally processed state. Iron ore and logs would be examples. Here the facilitator must remember that the easy procurement and ready availability is a very important issue to stress on.

Labour

In economics, labour (or labor) is a measure of the work

done by human beings. All human resources used in production constitute labour in respect of entrepreneurship. The facilitator should note that the availability of labour is to be stressed here. Who will do the work, how much will be the cost of labour etc. are the stress-points.

Skill

The facilitator should note that skill is the mental and physical ability to do a particular activity. Does the project demand high level skill? Can it be acquired?

Plant

This dimension depends upon the availability of technology at the local arena. Can the technology be acquired readily? Can it be kept running consistently?

After giving an orientation on the 5 inputs, ask the group to analyse each 5Q qualified ideas using the table given:

5 Input Analysis

Dimensions / Options	*Capital*	*Raw Material*	*Labour*	*Skill*	*Plant*	*Score*

Remember

The theme of scoring should be done on the availability of each dimension. Scoring will be done in a 4-Point Scale- easily available- 4; available- 3; hardly available- 2; not available- 1 For example

Dimensions / Options	*Capital*	*Raw Material*	*Labour*	*Skill*	*Plant*	*Score*
Candle Making	3	3	4	2	2	14
Poultry	4	3	3	3	4	17
Piggery	4	3	2	4	3	17
Handloom	2	3	3	3	4	15
Agarbatti	3	3	3	2	2	13
Artificial flowers	3	2	4	2	2	13
Carpet making	2	2	4	2	3	13

Tool No.3

Paired Comparison Analysis

The above analysis tool is useful in finding out just how well an option does in terms of the 5 inputs. But then, the sentiment and the consensus of the whole group members is also an important element in selecting a project. Therefore, yet another useful tool for prioritizing and selecting from an array of options can be administered using the paired comparison analysis.

Option	A	B	C	D	E	F	G	H
A:								
B:								
C:								
D:								
E:								
F:								
G:								
H:								

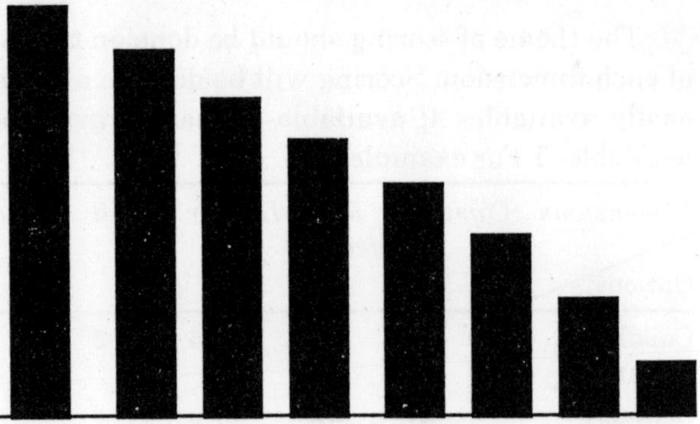

Option	Total	Rank
A:		
B:		
C:		
D:		
E:		
F:		
G:		
H:		

Considering the above example,

Option	*A: Candle Making*	*B: Poultry*	*C: Piggery*	*D: Handloom*	*E: Agarbatti*	*F: Artificial Flowers*	*G: Carpet*
A: Candle making		A	C	A	A	A	G
B: Poultry			C	B	E	B	B
C: Piggery				C	C	C	C
D: Handloom					E	D	D
E: Agarbatti						F	E
F: A.Flowers							G
G: Carpet							

The analysis is really simple

Taking the 1st row, the first cell need not be filled up as we do not have to compare 'candle making with candle making'. The 2nd cell is the comparison of option A: Candle Making and option B: Poultry and the decision is on option 'A'.

In the 2nd row, we see that the first two cells are blank. That is because comparison between A & B is already done and comparison between B & B is not needed.

In the 3rd row, A & C; B & C; are already done and C & C need not be compared.

In the 4th row, A & D; B & D; C & D are already done and D & D need not be compared. The same rule applies in the subsequent rows.

The compilation of the above analysis can be done as follows:

Option	*Total*	*Rank*
A:	4	2
B:	3	3
C:	6	1
D:	2	4
E:	3	3
F:	1	5
G:	2	4

The result can be now be interpreted as Option C: Piggery got the highest vote among the group members, followed by Option A: Candle Making.

What are the implications of these three analysis tools?

The 5Q Test is marketing-oriented analysis. It aims to

test the idea in the market. After all, marketing is the only dimension earning for the enterprise.

The 5 Input Tests is an intrinsic component test, aiming to test the potentiality of the option within the capacity of the enterprise.

The Paired Comparison Method used here is mainly to quantify the motivational degree between the options. However, care must be taken in comparing options. The facilitator should use this analysis to prioritize the suitable and economically viable options. Options with low score in the 5 Input Test should not be considered for comparison.

Do note that I have deviated from the conventional economic feasibility paradigm and have left out the most crucial component - Profitability test. I do believe that motivating and animating with words like "subsidy, loans, profits etc." would short-liven groups.

DEVELOPMENT PROGRAMME
For
EDUCATED YOUTHS

13

Sources of Business Ideas

There is no limit for sources of business ideas. Magazines, journals, sales brochures, newspapers, a walk on the street, watching TV programs, browsing over the internet, listing out daily issues, window shopping, a stroll in the city, reading books, sales emporiums trade fairs etc. The founder of Colorline, Bela Katrak quoted that she can identify various business opportunities just on her way to work. What really is needed is a proper mindset, attuning to business. Arya Kumar, Chief – Entrepreneurship Development & IPR Unit of BITS, Pilani at his National Entrepreneurship Network contribution, has identified the following:

Consumers

The final focal-point of the idea for a new product or service is Consumer and the needs of the consumers if taken into account can generate potentially sound ideas.

Existing Companies

A comprehensive analysis of competitive products & services already existing in the market may result in a new product with a better market appeal.

Distribution Channels

Members of the distribution channels are excellent

sources for new ideas because of their familiarity with the needs of the market.

Government

Government can be a source of new product ideas in two ways:

- The files of the Patent Office contain numerous new product possibilities.
- New product ideas can come in response to govt. regulations.

14

Project Report Writing

It is always good for the facilitator be equipped with a basic knowledge of how project reports should be written. Various authorities and organizations stress different formats but at the bottom line, the following are the main components in every format. It should be noted that to write an effective project report, one has to be well-versed in the project. Intensive and extensive research have to be done beforehand. As an add-on, these project reports can serve as a business plan, a blue-print of entrepreneurship. The following are the main components of a good project report. *All of the chapters/sections may not be required in writing a particular project, but are described here nonetheless for comprehensive sake.*

I. Organization Description

Mission Statement
Summary of Activity to Date
Current Stage of Development
Competencies
Product or Service
Description
Benefits to customer
Differences from current offerings

Objectives
Keys to Success
Location and Facilities.

II. Business Analysis

Entry Barriers
Supply and Distribution
Technological Factors
Seasonality
Economic Influences
Regulatory Issues.

III. Market Analysis

Definition of Overall Market
Market Size and Growth
Market Trends
Market Segments
Targeted Segments
Customer Characteristics
Customer Needs
Purchasing Decision Process
Product Positioning.

IV. Competition

Profiles of Primary Competitors
Competitors' Products/Services & Market Share
Competitive Evaluation of Product
Distinct Competitive Advantage
Competitive Weaknesses
Future Competitors.

V. Marketing and Sales

Products Offered
Pricing
Distribution
Promotion

Advertising and Publicity
Trade Shows
Partnerships
Discounts and Incentives
Sales Force
Sales Forecasts.

VI. Operations

Product Development
Development Team
Development Costs
Development Risks
Manufacturing (if applicable)
Production Processes
Production Equipment
Quality Assurance
Administration
Key Suppliers
Product / Service Delivery
Customer Service and Support
Human Resource Plan
Facilities.

VII. Management and Organization

Management Team
Open Positions
Board of Directors
Key Personnel
Organizational Chart.

VIII. Risks and Contingencies

Some common risks include:
Increased competition
Loss of a key employee
Suppliers' failure to meet deadlines

Regulatory changes
Change in business conditions.

XI. Financial Projections

Assumptions (date of commencement, commission, tax rate,
average inventory, sales forecast, etc.)
Financial Statements (Balance Sheet, Income Statement, Cash Flow Statement)
Break Even Analysis
Key Ratio Projections (quick ratio, current ratio, D/E, D/A,
ROE, ROA, working capital)
Financial Resources
Financial Strategy.

XII. Summary and Conclusions

The following project report was prepared using the business opportunity identified by the former SIRD Director, Pu Zothankuma MCS and was submitted for possible coordinated State-wide self help group project to Pu Vanhela Pachuau IAS, the then-Secretary, Rural Development Department: Government of Mizoram.

REPORT ON BAMBOO CHIPPING

Prepared by:

LALDINLIANA
Asst. Director / Core Faculty (Commerce)
State Institute of Rural Development
Mizoram : Kolasib

To

The Director
State Institute of Rural Development
Mizoram : Kolasib

Subject : Submission of project report

Sir,

I beg to state that the assignment of formulating a project report on bamboo chipping is completed and submitted accordingly for your kind scrutiny. I would like to mention that the following activities have been made for the completion of the report-

1. Visit to the site where the bamboo chipper is kept. It was shifted from Sairang to EPIP-Lengte, which is about 5 kilometres from Lengpui Airport main road.
2. Information regarding the negotiated rate between Hindustan Paper Corporation, Panchgram-Assam and Government of Mizoram was obtained from the concerned officer. Further information regarding the marketing of bamboo chips to Bangladesh at the rate of $ 32 per metric ton and the capacity of truckloads, which is bamboo 8 quintals and chips 16 quintals was also obtained. These information are not reflected in the project report as export to Bangladesh at such a rate is not feasible and the load capacity is irrational.
3. Royalty and permit factor was conveyed by the DFO, Forest & Environment Department. Further clarification and specific rates will have to be obtained at the turn-key stage.

Please revert for any other issues.

Sincerely,

(LALDINLIANA)
Asst. Director / Core Faculty
State Institute of Rural Development

General Information

The project is intended to provide entrepreneurial activity for the Self-Help Groups (SHGs) within Mizoram. As far as organizational structure is concerned, the SHGs are rural microenterprises functioning with the facilitation of NGOs and other development agencies. The central activity for the project is to produce processed raw material for the already identified market in the form of bamboo chippings.

Project Description

The main capital expenditure will be incurred in the procuring of the chipper machine. The machine identified is local-made. It is basically a cylindrical wheel with trays on its circumference to accommodate pre-cut bamboo of about 1.5 feet in length. The wheel has a diameter of around 2.5 feet and has 4 trays. The wheel is fitted on a steel frame structure with motor-driven blades fixed in such a way that when the wheel is rotated, it slices the bamboo into rings which is collected and then manually flattened into chips. The main steel frame is around 3 x 2 feet standing at a height of 3 feet. The machine is automated by three motors for running the blade and rotating the wheel-tray. The photographs of the proposed machine can be seen as below:

As seen in the photographs, the machine does not occupy much space, which means that the work-shed need not be a big building, and is estimated around Rs. 40,000/-. The structure without the motors and blades cost around Rs 26,000/- approximately and is designed by our contact.

Apart from the machine itself, containment for the bamboo chips for packing and carrying should be purchased. A number of gunny-bags or jute bags will have to be provided for this purpose. Installation charges will also be borne as capital expenditure. Electrification of the work-shed will also be capitalized. A supply of water to wet the blades should be arranged in the work-shed. The bamboo-dust will also have to be housed properly so that it can also be sold as by-products.

As for the collection of raw material, permit will have to be obtained from Forest & Environment Department, Government of Mizoram and royalty should be paid for the same as per existing rule.

Transportation of bamboo chips will have to be arranged from the facilitating agencies/ authorities. Arrangements with logistics industries in Mizoram e.g. Road King, Eastern Trading etc. whose trucks always return to Assam unladened with cargo would be a feasible option.

To make the project economically viable, at least 64 units should be in operational to meet the 50 tons requirement market feed. The following table shows the variables in their established values.

---

1 Bamboo is estimated to weigh 3 kgs.

1 Bamboo can be purchased at the rate of Rs. 6 (present market rate)

1 Unit should be able to have an output of 0.78 ton per day for optimum production, which means 64 units will have an approximate output of 50 tons

Taking the above matrix, 260 bamboos is needed for 0.78 ton output per day

---

The capital expenditure for 1 **unit** can be estimated as below:

Serial No.	*Items*	*Amount*
1	8 Chipper machines @ Rs. 40,000 p.p.	40,000
2	Gunny/ Jute bags	1,250
3	Electrification and provisions	1,250
	Total	42,500

The cost of the project for one unit in terms of capital items comes to the amount of Rupees Forty Two Thousand and Five Hundred.

Assumptions

Here we assume that the raw material supply is consistent. We assume that the power supply is adequate and consistent.

Critical Points

It should be noted that the cost of *mau* of 12 feet long is sold at Rs. 6/- at present. Two other varieties, *rawnal* and *rua* are priced at Rs. 8/- and Rs. 10/- respectively. Therefore, the raw-material cost will differ accordingly with the usage of the variety.

Since the cost of royalty and permit is not yet identifiable, it will be another factor that will disrupt the analysis.

Market Plan

As far as the market plan is concerned, verbal negotiations have been made with Hindustan Paper Corporation (HPC), Panchgram: Assam. As per discussion with the Executive Director, the HPC would be willing to purchase from the project at least 50 metric tons per day. The whole requirement of the HPC plant would come around 1,100 metric tons per day. Therefore, it can be safely said that the whole output from this project can be absorbed by HPC. It would be a case of Demand > Supply in our situation.

The Executive Director made a statement that the Corporation would be willing to buy the chips at *cost plus 5%.* This price will have to be contested with the rate already negotiated with the Industries Department, Government of Mizoram which is Rs. 2.40/- per kg or Rs. 2,400/- per ton:

Capital Requirements and Costs

We have already identified that for one unit, the capital requirements would come to Rs.42,500/-. Therefore, *the project capital requirement for the whole State i.e. 64 units will amount to Rs. 27,20,000/-*

Operating Requirements Costs

Serial No.	*Description*	*Monthly Estimation*
1	Electricity	300
2	Wages @ Rs. 3000 for 2 personnel	6,000
3	Depreciation	500
4	Raw Material 260 bamboos @ Rs. 6/- p.p.	39,000
	TOTAL	45,800

Note: Depreciation is calculated using **Straight-Line Method,** assuming that the machine will have an operation life of 5 years. The value will be reduced to a negligible scrap-value after the expiry of 5 years. The working will be as follows-

Book-Value of the machine = Rs. 40,000
Scrap-Value = Rs. 10,000
Life expectancy = 5 years

$$\text{Depreciation} = \frac{\text{Book Value} - \text{Scrap Value}}{\text{Life Expected}}$$

$$= \frac{\text{Rs. } 40{,}000 - \text{Rs. } 10{,}000}{5 \text{ yrs.}}$$

= Rs. 6000 per annum

= **Rs. 500 per month**

Financial Analysis

The projected month-wise Trading, Profit & Loss Account for one unit can be displayed as below:

Trading account

Debit					Credit
	Particulars	*Amount*		*Particulars*	*Amount*
To	Wages for 2 personnel @ Rs. 3000 per month	6,000	By	Sales of 19.5 tons @ Rs. 2,400	46,800
	Power	300			
	Raw Material 260 bamboos @ Rs. 6 for 25 days	39,000			
	Gross Profit	1,500			
		46,800			46,800

Profit & Loss Account

Depreciation	500	Gross Profit	1,500
Net Profit	1,000	b/d	
	1,500		1,500

Trading Account is concerned with all the direct expenses and incomes of the project. Direct wages, rent of the work-shed, power consumption for production constitutes the direct expenditures.

The month-wise cost of production of one kilogram of bamboo chips for one (1) unit can be calculated as -

Serial No.	*Particulars*	*Amount*
1	Raw Material 260 bamboos per day @ Rs. 6 for 25 days	39,000
2	Power	300
3	Wages @ Rs. 3000 for 2 personnel	6,000
4	Depreciation @ 20%	500
	TOTAL	45,800

Therefore, the cost of production will be:

$$\text{Rs. } \frac{45{,}800 \times 1/1000}{19.50 \text{ tons}} = \text{Rs. } 2.34$$

Economic Analysis

Break-Even Point

BEP =Fixed Cost/ Sales – Variable Costs X100

In the project, three elements can be identified as Fixed Costs, namely-

Depreciation = Rs. 500

Wages = Rs. 6,000

Here Depreciation and Direct Wages are treated as Fixed Costs as we assume that the supply of raw material and operation to be constant and not dependent on work-load. Therefore, **Fixed Cost will amount to Rs. 6,500.**

Variable cost can be calculated by adding raw material requirement Rs. 39,000; Power consumption Rs. 300. Thus, the **Variable Cost will amount to Rs. 39,300.**

BEP = 6,500/ 46,800 – 39,300 X 100

= **86%**

Interpretation of BEP

By the sale of 83% of the whole output, the project will break even with no loss or profit. Increase of sales beyond this point will earn profit.

Pay-Back Period

$$PBP = \frac{\text{Total Investment}}{\text{Profit per month}}$$

$$= \frac{\text{Rs. } 40{,}000 + 1250 + 1250}{\text{Rs. } 1000}$$

$$= 42.5 \text{ X } 1/12 \text{ months}$$

$$= 3.54$$

Interpretation of PBP

The project will pay itself back in 3 years, 6 months and 13 days

As mentioned before, the project is feasible because production is demand-based. In fact, the feeder market is already allocated which makes it viable.

Optimum Analysis

As mentioned before, the optimum outlay can be achieved with 64 units installed. The rationale can be seen stated as per the requirement of the market, at least 50 tons is in demand per day. Since one unit can produce 0.78 ton per day at its optimum level, 64 units could produce approximately 50 tons per day. The following analysis can give a picture if 64 units are operational simultaneously.

A month-wise Trading, Profit & Loss Account with **64 units** can be projected as follows

Trading account

Debit | **Credit**

	Particulars	*Amount*		*Particulars*	*Amount*
To	Wages for 128 personnel @ Rs 3000 per month	3,84,000	By	Sales of 50 tons @ Rs. 2400/- per ton X 25 days	30,00,000
	Power	19,200			
	Raw Material of 16,640 bamboos @ Rs. 6/- per bamboo x 25 Days	24,96,000			
	Gross Profit c/d	1,00,800			
		30,00,000			30,00,000

Profit & Loss Account

Particulars	Amount	Particulars	Amount
Depreciation	32,000	Gross Profit b/d	1,00,800
Net Profit	**68,800**		
	1,00,800		1,00,800

If we are given the **cost plus profit margin of 5%** price, we would be having a market price of Rs. 2.46. This would give a profit of Rs.0.12 per kg and naturally enhance the net profit to **Rs. 1,43,800/-**

Conclusion

The project can be made a reality only with proper networking of SHGs in the district. All the calculations are made to the matrix of one district only. To get the figure for the whole State, compounding the relevant variables with the number of districts should be done. It should be noted that critical variables like royalty, permit, and carriage outward expenses are still not incorporated in the calculations. These variables can change the interpretations and presentations. Also, improvement can be made with the machinery design. The present machine processes only pre-cut bamboos. Cutting the bamboos to fit the tray, again, will be labour extensive.

15

Facilitating Financial Management Skills

One of the most crucial dimensions needed to be facilitated to the Self Help Groups is the management of finance. Thus, facilitation of financial statement preparation is called for. Financial statement may be defined as a written report that summarizes an organization's accounting data and indicate its financial condition/ position. It highlights the financial health of the organization and form the basis of financial reporting.

Assumptions underlying preparation of Financial Statements may be highlighted into three basic principles.

1. **Accrual basis-** Transactions are recognized when they occur and not when cash is paid or received.
2. **Going Concern-** It is assumed that enterprise will continue its operations.
3. **Consistency** of accounting policies and standards used

Types of Financial Statements

Profit and Loss Account/ Income Statement

The income statement provides a financial summary of

the organization's operating results during a specified period. Operating income /expenses are those that are earned /spent in the normal course of business. In Income statement, Non-operating Income/Expense are also considered. Although Income Statement is prepared annually for reporting purposes, they are generally worked out on monthly basis (even fortnightly in case of start ups) by management.

Illustration

Income Statement for XYZ for the year ended March 31st, 2008

	Particulars	*Amount (Rs)*
1	Sales	1,00,000
2	Less: Cost of Goods Sold	25,000
3	GROSS PROFIT	75,000
4	Less: Salary	20,000
5	Less: Depreciation	10,000
6	Add: Profit from sale of asset*	10,000
7	Less: Interest paid on debt	20,000
8	PROFIT BEFORE TAX	35,000
9	Less: Tax @ 30%	10,500
10	PROFIT AFTER TAX/ NET PROFIT	24,500

Entries that are transferred from Income Statement to Balance Sheet:

Profit that remains with the organization after distribution of profits is called **Retained Earnings** and is transferred to the Balance Sheet and is added to the capital account of the SHGs.

Balance Sheet

The balance sheet presents a summary of the

organization's financial position at a given point of time. It depicts what organizations *owns (ASSETS)* and what it *owes (LIABILITIES)* to others. Thus it provides a financial position of a venture at a given point of time

Illustration

Balance Sheet of XYZ as on March 31, 2008

Liabilities	*(Rs)*	*Assets*	*(Rs)*
Current	Liabilities	Current	Assets
Current Liabilities		Current Assets	
Short Term Loan	10,000	Cash	20,000
Accounts payable	15,000	Accounts Receivable	30,000
		Stock	10,000
Corpus Fund	4,00,000	Plant	1,50,000
		Machinery	2,15,000
	4,25,000		**4,25,000**

Bibliography

Adiar, John: *Decision Making & Problem Solving Strategies*, Kogan Page India, 2009

Adiar, John: *Leadership for Innovation*, Kogan Page India, 2008

Buzan, T: *Use Your Head*, BBC Publications, London, 1974

Coulter, Mary: *Entrepreneurship in Action*, Prentice Hall India, 2005

Dawson, R: *Make the Right Decision Every Time*, Nicholas Brealey, London, 1994

De Bono, E: *The Five Day Course in Thinking*, McGraw-Hill, Maidenhead, 1968

De Bono, E: *The Use of Lateral Thinking*, Penguin, London, 1971

Elizabeth Christopher: *Leadership Training*, Viva Books, 2002

Hart, Lois B: *Faultless Facilitation – A Sourcebook of Activites*, Viva Books, 2002

Hundal, PS: A Study on Entrepreneurial Motivation, *Journal of Applied Psychology*, Vol 55, 1971

Jones, Ken: *Icebreakers*, Viva Books, 2000

Kashyap, P & Raul, S: *The Rural Marketing Handbook*, Dreamtech Press, 2007

Khanka, SS: *Entrepreneurial Development*, S Chand, 2005

Khanna, S & Dwan, U: *Rural Development Strategies and Planning*, Sonali Publication, 2003

Koestler, A: *The Act of Creation*, Hutchinson, London, 1964

Mahmud, Abdul Aziz: Developing Effective Indigenous Entrepreneurs, *Malaysian Management Review*, April 1974

Newstrom, JW & Scannell, EE: *Games Trainers Play*, Tata McGraw-Hill, 2006

NIRD-NERC: *Participatory Approach on Development Programmes*, 2003

NREGP Report: www.nrega.nic.in 2007

Rawlinson, JG: *Creative Thinking and Brainstorming*, Gower, Aldershot, 1983

Vepa, RK: *Entrepreneurship for Development of Backward Areas*, National Productivity Council, New Delhi, 1973

Wigneraja, P: *Participatory Development- Learning from South Asia*, UNU Press, 1991

Websites for Entreprenurs

AllBusiness.com: Champions of Small Business - www.allbusiness.com

Byplans.com: The Planning People - www.bplans.com

Entrepreneur Magazine - www.entrepreneurmag.com

eweb – www.eweb.slu.edu/default.htm

Fambiz.com - www.fambiz.com

Forum for Women Entrepreneur - www.fwe.org

Idea Café - www.ideacafe.com

Mind Tools - www.mindtools.com

MoreBusiness: By Entrepreneurs, For Entrepreneurs - www.morebusiness.com

National Entrepreneurship Network - www.nenonline.com

The Business Forum Online - www.businessforum.com

The Entrepreneur's Mind - www.benlore.com

Young Entrepreneurs' Organisation - www.yeo.org

Index

■■■